THE ART OF PHILIP LARKIN

SYDNEY STUDIES IN LITERATURE

FOUNDING EDITOR (1965–7): the late Professor K. G. W. Cross, then Head of the English Department, University of Newcastle

GENERAL EDITORS (1967–   ): G. A. Wilkes, Challis Professor of English Literature and Dr A. P. Riemer, Associate Professor of English Literature, University of Sydney

THE ART OF PHILIP LARKIN
by Simon Petch

HENRY FIELDING'S *TOM JONES*
by Anthony J. Hassall

JAMES JOYCE'S *ULYSSES* (*out of print*)
by Clive Hart

JANE AUSTEN'S *EMMA*
by J. F. Burrows

THE MAJOR POEMS OF JOHN KEATS
by Norman Talbot

MILTON'S *PARADISE LOST*
by Michael Wilding

THE POETRY OF ROBERT LOWELL
by Vivian Smith

A READING OF SHAKESPEARE'S *ANTONY AND CLEOPATRA*
by A. P. Riemer

SHAKESPEARE'S *HAMLET*
by Derick R. Marsh

THE ART OF
PHILIP LARKIN

SIMON PETCH
Senior Lecturer in English
University of Sydney

SYDNEY UNIVERSITY PRESS

SYDNEY UNIVERSITY PRESS
Press Building, University of Sydney

UNITED KINGDOM, EUROPE, MIDDLE EAST, AFRICA
Eurospan Limited
3 Henrietta Street, London WC2E 8LU

NORTH AND SOUTH AMERICA
International Scholarly Book Services, Inc.
P.O. Box 1632, Beaverton, OR 97075, U.S.A.

National Library of Australia Cataloguing-in-Publication data

Petch, Simon.
　The art of Philip Larkin.

　(Sydney studies in literature)
　ISBN 0 424 00090 3

　1. Larkin, Philip—Criticism and
　interpretation. I. Title. (Series)

821.914

First published 1981
© Simon Petch 1981

Printed in Australia by Macarthur Press (Books) Pty Limited, Parramatta

CONTENTS

ACKNOWLEDGEMENTS

Works by Philip Larkin: extracts from *Jill*, *A Girl in Winter*, *The North Ship*, and *The Whitsun Weddings* are reprinted by permission of Faber and Faber Ltd. Extracts from *High Windows* (copyright © 1974 by Philip Larkin) are reprinted by permission of Faber and Faber Ltd and Farrar, Straus & Giroux, Inc. Quotations from 'Deceptions', 'Triple Time', 'Next, Please', 'Wires', 'Poetry of Departures', 'Skin', 'If, My Darling', 'Spring', 'Lines on a Young Lady's Photograph Album', 'Reasons for Attendance', 'Church Going', and 'At Grass' are reprinted from *The Less Deceived* by permission of The Marvell Press, England.

Critical and scholarly material: I am grateful to David Timms for allowing me to quote freely from his book *Philip Larkin* (Oliver & Boyd), to Roger Day and the Open University for allowing me to quote from his course unit *Philip Larkin* (The Open University Press), and to Robert Langbaum for allowing me to quote from his book *The Modern Spirit* (Chatto & Windus). Edward Arnold has given me permission to quote from *The Ironic Harvest* by Geoffrey Thurley. Oxford University Press has allowed me to quote from *The New Poets* by M. L. Rosenthal, and quotations from *Eight Contemporary Poets* by Calvin Bedient are also reprinted by permission of Oxford University Press. Vision Press, London, has permitted me to quote from *Lost Bearings in English Poetry* by David Holbrook, and Mouton and Co., The Hague, has permitted me to quote from *An Uncommon Poet for the Common Man* by Lolette Kuby. The quotation from p. 21 of A. Alvarez's introduction to *The New Poetry* (copyright © Penguin Books Ltd, 1962) is reprinted by permission of Penguin Books Ltd, and the quotations from pp. 14 and 44 of *The Situation of Poetry: Contemporary Poetry and Its Traditions* by Robert Pinsky (copyright © 1976 by Princeton University Press) are reprinted by permission of Princeton University Press. Full references to other material quoted or referred to are given in the notes.

PREFACE

This book is aimed at readers new to Larkin as well as at those familiar with his work. It attempts to provide the scope of an introduction, and also to examine in detail some of the problems that have emerged from criticism of Larkin's poetry. It was written in the belief that the great achievement of Larkin's poetry is its astonishing capacity to focus persistently and penetratingly on central aspects of human life in ways that are comprehensible and accessible without being either shallow or condescending, and without ignoring what Yeats called 'the fascination of what's difficult'. This, to my mind, is what constitutes Larkin's genius.

This view is of course not universal, and previous criticism, as well as my debts to and divergences from it, is reviewed in the introduction. Thereafter, following a glance at Larkin's early work as novelist as well as a poet, each chapter is devoted to a study of each of Larkin's volumes of poetry. All too rarely, I think, have the techniques of Larkin's poetry received the sustained and developed analysis they demand. My own discussion is largely dependent on such analysis, in which I have tried to say things that have not been said before. Because my main concern is with poetic technique I have nothing to say about Larkin's life. Blake Morrison's recently published *The Movement: English Poetry and Fiction of the 1950s*[1] promises to be a thoroughgoing study of the milieu in which Larkin began to write, and in any case that milieu is adequately treated in David Timms' *Philip Larkin.*[2] I have merely touched on Larkin's jazz writing and his scattered essays and reviews where they have been particularly relevant to my argument. In some ways this is regrettable. In a recent interview Larkin has acknowledged jazz and dance music as 'a kind of folk poetry'[3] that shaped his own aesthetic; but if this influence is

---

[1] Oxford University Press, 1980.
[2] Oliver & Boyd, Edinburgh 1973.
[3] *The Observer*, 16 December 1979, p. 35.

to be analysed fully, the jazz writing deserves its own study, and the same can be said of Larkin's literary journalism, which, as B. C. Bloomfield's recent bibliography suggests,[4] is now getting voluminous.

Above all I wish to show how the accessibility with which Larkin's poetry has frequently been credited is earned; that it is dependent on a particularly manipulative manner as much as on familiarity of subject-matter. The 'authority of sadness'[5] is a phrase that Larkin has used of Stevie Smith's poems, but it is also strikingly appropriate to his own work; and if his 'sadness' has received more than its fair share of critical attention, his 'authority' has received decidedly less. One purpose of this book is to redress the balance of critical emphasis. The strategies of Larkin's poetry are often based upon the firm and decisive establishment of an unobtrusive authorial presence whose function is to manipulate the reader's perspective. However impalpable the design of a poem, and however indirectly we perceive it, such a presence is an essential precondition of the readiness with which we respond to Larkin's poetry. I have tried to focus on its various manifestations. Without getting embroiled in Larkin's politics, it is enough here to suggest a relationship between his own right-wing beliefs as a version of Dr Johnson's high Toryism, and this neo-Augustan aspect of his verse. More generally, an attempt has been made to give a sense of Larkin's development as a writer by looking at the blending of his concerns with his strategies, and by examining the intricate patterns of form and content woven in the texture of the poetry.

The final thing to be said about this book is that its subject will probably dislike it. According to Philip Larkin 'there are only three legitimate things that anyone can do with poetry—write it, read it, or publish it',[6] and he rarely bypasses an opportunity to lambast what he has called 'a critical industry which is concerned with culture in the abstract'.[7] It is undeniable that the most pernicious effect of modernism, as a critical no less than a literary movement, has been to drive literature exclusively into the universities. To give my own work the aura of 'legitimacy' I have kept it as far from 'abstraction' as possible by relying extensively on detailed discussion of particular poems, and by discussing the poetry as far as possible in terms appropriate to itself rather than to sociology, psychology, philosophy, or economic history. I have tried constantly to bear in mind Larkin's own high valuation of 'the essential

[4] *Philip Larkin: A Bibliography 1933–1976*, Faber and Faber, London 1979.
[5] *New Statesman*, 64 (July–December 1962), p. 418.
[6] Interview on the sleeve of the recording of *The Less Deceived*.
[7] Interview with Ian Hamilton, *The London Magazine*, 4 (November 1964), p. 71.

nexus between reader and writer',[8] and my intention has always been to send my own reader back to the poems.

University of Sydney   SIMON PETCH
May 1980

POSTSCRIPT

Since this book was substantially completed, two interviews given by Larkin have appeared in print: in *The Observer* (16 December 1979), and in *The London Magazine* (April/May 1980). Although the former is mentioned in the Preface and the latter is referred to briefly in Chapter II, I have not been able to make full use of either.

[8] *Observer* interview, p. 35.

EDITIONS

References to works by Philip Larkin are to the following editions, and have been placed in the text.

NOVELS

Jill. Faber and Faber, London 1975. (First published by the Fortune Press in 1946.)
A Girl in Winter. Faber and Faber, London 1975. (First published 1947.)

POEMS

The North Ship. Faber and Faber, London 1966. (First published by the Fortune Press in 1945.)
The Less Deceived. The Marvell Press, Hessle, East Yorkshire 1955. (This press is now located in London.)
The Whitsun Weddings. Faber and Faber, London 1964.
High Windows. Faber and Faber, London 1974.

Full references to Larkin's essays, reviews, and articles, are given in the notes. For additional information on Larkin's writings, readers should consult B. C. Bloomfield, *Philip Larkin: A Bibliography 1933–1976* (Faber and Faber, London 1979).

Introduction

Larkin and the Critics

On 9 September 1960, the *Times Literary Supplement* carried an additional supplement entitled 'The British Imagination: Trenchancy and Tradition'. Its poetry section, ominously headed 'Signs of an All too Correct Compassion', included an identikit portrait of a contemporary 'composite poet':

> He prefers, on the whole, traditional metres and stanza forms to formal experiment. His diction is that of spoken speech, perhaps a little distanced and formalized, rather than that of song, oratory, or tragic harangue. He confronts difficult emotional situations with a technique of controlled relaxation. He likes to pursue an argument through a poem. He will often tell a little anecdote with an implicit moral. He likes domestic episodes and snapshot views. He distrusts the picturesque. He is more interested in discussing types than individuals. His strong lines are those which express a cogent generalization rather than those which isolate a particular perception. He is rather weak, on the whole, on visual imagery, a townsman rather than a countryman. He has often a touch of humour or wit, but it is subdued and subacid rather than boisterous or exuberant.

Although Larkin is not mentioned in these sentences, he haunts them; for elsewhere in the essay he is frequently cited as an example of the deficiencies of the British imagination. Thus he is compared unfavourably with the Americans Richard Wilbur and Robert Creeley as 'too literary', the somewhat negative virtues of Larkin's poetry being akin to those listed in this passage. And while this passage would be woefully inadequate even as a superficial description of Larkin's manner, the writer's patronizing attitude to his 'composite poet' (as well as his constant use of Larkin to exemplify British poetry) is representative of a persistent trend in critical attitudes towards Larkin generally. Specifically, the essay raises

1

two points that have become central to criticism of Larkin: he is representatively English; and in being so he has shut himself off from more adventurous movements and developments in American poetry.

The date of this essay should be remembered, for hardly has a new decade begun than we can see the 'fifties being moulded into myth. The early appearance of Larkin's work in D. J. Enright's anthology *Poets of the 1950s*[1] may have been unfortunate, for in many ways Larkin's critics have been reluctant to let him out of that decade. Thus A. R. Jones said confidently, in 1962: 'it is in the poetry of Philip Larkin that the spirit of the 1950s finds its most complete expression in English poetry';[2] and the second part of Jones' title, 'A Note on Transatlantic Culture', keeps Larkin planted firmly on English soil. Similarly John Press's survey *A Map of Modern English Verse*[3] confined Larkin to the chapter 'The Movement and Poets of the 1950s', and in 'Philip Larkin of England'[4] A. K. Weatherhead reminded the readers of his American journal exactly where Larkin did belong. But Weatherhead's article came almost a decade later than that of Jones, and as time has gone by and Larkin has continued to write it has become increasingly difficult to keep him in the 'fifties. He has thus been reclassified as the poet of the contemporary (English) scene. Lolette Kuby tells us, sympathetically if unhelpfully, that Larkin's poetic *personae* are products of 'the mid-twentieth century, in which Larkin sees the inherent tragedy of the human condition, in other eras diffused and diluted, gathered to a head, condensed and dramatized in the daily life of the average man'.[5] These notes, and variations on them, have been struck by debunkers and apologists alike. Thus Charles Tomlinson, snarling at 'the ingratiating image of the average man', complains about Larkin's 'intense parochialism'.[6] Alvarez diagnoses Larkin's disease as the peculiarly English one of 'gentility', by which he apparently means complacency: 'a belief that life is always more or less orderly, people always more or less polite, their emotions and habits more or less decent and more or less controllable; that God, in short, is more or

[1] D. J. Enright (ed.), *Poets of the 1950s*, The Kenkyusha Press, Tokyo 1955.
[2] A. R. Jones, 'The Poetry of Philip Larkin: A Note on Transatlantic Culture', *Western Humanities Review*, 16 (1962), p. 145.
[3] John Press, *A Map of Modern English Verse*, Oxford University Press, London 1969, pp. 251–70.
[4] A. K. Weatherhead, 'Philip Larkin of England', *ELH*, 38 (1971).
[5] Lolette Kuby, *An Uncommon Poet for the Common Man*, Mouton, The Hague 1974, p. 14.
[6] Charles Tomlinson, 'The Middlebrow Muse', *Essays in Criticism*, 7 (1957), pp. 208, 214.

less good'.[7] And David Holbrook uses the same concept of gentility to categorize both Larkin's language and his detachment, for Holbrook regards Larkin's limitations as general examples of inadequate 'day-to-day attitudes to existence in our civilization'.[8] All these people have their various solutions and remedies for poetry: to Tomlinson's mind, a sense of objectivity is what is needed; Alvarez prescribes a stiff dose of Berryman and Lowell; and Holbrook advocates transcendence as the one thing needful. Larkin supplies none of these.

Weatherhead also explains Larkin's moods and attitudes by reference to English culture, although he does so from a more sympathetic standpoint than Holbrook. Recently in England, he tells us, 'the glorious and the flamboyant have gradually been edged out of life, corporate and private, in favour of the safe, reasonable step, the considered decision, the committee report; it is as though Britain realized that it had lost its youth and was determined to be sensible, to watch its weight and its savings, and not catch cold'.[9] For better or worse the poet and his culture prove each other, and both remain on their own side of the Atlantic. And thus a reviewer of Larkin's more recent book, *High Windows*, went out of his way to stress 'how alien is the lucid, complexly sentenced, tonal and sardonic character of Larkin's poetry to that of the most highly-reputed contemporary American work'.[10]

For Donald Davie, too, Larkin represents 'British poetry at the point where it has least in common with American, a poetry which consciously repudiates the assumptions, and the liberties, which American poets take for granted'.[11] Davie at least tries to see Larkin's poetry in some wider perspective than that of the post-war years, yet his thesis—that Hardy is the most far-reaching influence of the past half-century and that Larkin is his natural heir—is offered as little more than an apology. His admiration for Hardy, which emerges strongly from his discussion of particular poems, is offset by his regret at Hardy's refusal to be transcendent: 'his poems, instead of transforming and displacing quantifiable reality or the reality of common sense, are on the contrary just so many glosses on that reality, which is conceived of as unchallengeably "given" and final'. Politically, therefore, Hardy is to be seen as liberal

[7] A. Alvarez (ed.), *The New Poetry*, Penguin Books, Harmondsworth 1962, p. 21.
[8] David Holbrook, *Lost Bearings in English Poetry*, Vision Press, London 1977, p. 11.
[9] Weatherhead, 'Philip Larkin of England', p. 617.
[10] W. H. Pritchard, 'Larkin Lives', *Hudson Review*, 28 (1975–6), p. 307.
[11] Donald Davie, *Thomas Hardy and British Poetry*, Routledge and Kegan Paul, London 1973, p. 188.

rather than radical; and for Davie, Hardy the poet 'sold the vocation short, tacitly surrendering the proudest claims traditionally made for the act of the poetic imagination'.[12] The same objection, of course, is levelled at Larkin. But Hardy's refusal to don the vatic mantle and give us an alternative reality should surely not be seen as a 'surrender', for while he does keep his feet on the ground and never loses sight of the world of all of us—the world where, as Wordsworth knew, in the end we find our happiness or not at all—his poems do frequently change or modify our perceptions of actualities. Hardy has indeed been important to Larkin, as we shall see, but the main aspect of Hardy's distinctive contribution to twentieth-century poetry is his idiosyncratic manipulation of language, his moulding of different kinds of linguistic usage into a usable, composite form. This has been well characterized by the American poet Robert Pinsky as 'bringing elegance and formality into an ironic, hesitant relation with bluntness and strain',[13] its treatment of compound states of feeling is capable of transforming the way reality is perceived even if it does not quite 'displace' reality (whatever that means), and it is a legacy bequeathed to American as well as to British poets.

For Davie, therefore, Larkin is a poet of 'lowered sights and patiently diminished expectations',[14] and if Davie sells Larkin short in this he nevertheless performs a valuable service by suggesting that the reasons for Larkin's manner pre-date the 1950s. Other critics have tried to liberate Larkin from the contemporary, and to see him in a broader context. 'His allegiances are with the nineteenth century',[15] says Christopher Ricks in a review of *The Whitsun Weddings*, mentioning Wordsworth, Hardy and Tennyson. Reviewing *High Windows*, John Bayley sees Larkin's 'poetry of artificial arrest'[16] as a logical development of the manner of Keats and Tennyson. J. R. Watson[17] adds Browning to these names, and Lolette Kuby throws in Jonson and Praed.[18] While this sort of thing does have the virtue of drawing attention to the sheer variety of this very unprofuse poet, it is ultimately meaningless; and thus we find Seamus Heaney giving us an *Everyman* Larkin, a Skelton Larkin, a Cavalier Larkin, a late

[12] Davie, *Thomas Hardy*, p. 62.
[13] Robert Pinsky, *The Situation of Poetry: Contemporary Poetry and its Traditions*, Princeton University Press, 1976, p. 44.
[14] Davie, *Thomas Hardy*, p. 71.
[15] C. Ricks, 'The Whitsun Weddings', *Phoenix*, 11/12 (Autumn-Winter 1973–4, Philip Larkin issue), p. 6. First printed as 'A True Poet', *NYRB*, 14 January 1965, pp. 10–11. Subsequent page references will be to *Phoenix*.
[16] John Bayley, 'Too Good for This World', *TLS*, 21 June 1974, p. 654.
[17] J. R. Watson, 'The Other Larkin', *Critical Quarterly*, 17 (1975), p. 348.
[18] Kuby, *An Uncommon Poet*, ch. 1.

Augustan Larkin, a Tennysonesque and a Hardyesque Larkin, an Imagist Larkin, a Hopkinsian Larkin, a Shakespearean Larkin, and finally a seaside-postcard Larkin, all within three pages[19] — an altogether different 'composite poet' from the one pieced together by the *Times Literary Supplement* in 1960. In the light of these conflicting accounts we should find it necessary to enquire into what makes Larkin distinctly himself rather than *any* kind of composite poet, or 'the unofficial laureate of post-war Britain',[20] or a latter-day Hardy. For no poet is ever just an extension of or spokesman for his culture any more than he is an amalgamation of other styles and influences, and we have it on the authority of Robert Lowell that even in the 1950s Larkin was an innovator who made other styles obsolete: 'No style or school could have given his words their poignant severity'.[21]

If we now turn to Larkin's own comments on poetry, it becomes immediately apparent that the most important fact about his approach to poetry is his firmly explicit anti-modernist stance. While he may or may not remind us of Tennyson, Hardy, or Browning, he hardly reminds us stylistically of Pound or Eliot. He has professed admiration for Betjeman, 'a poet for whom the modern poetic revolution has simply not taken place', and 'the living contradiction of Eliot's contention that the better the poet, the more complete the separation between the man who suffers and the man who creates'. Thus Betjeman's work has escaped 'the aberration of modernism, that blighted all the arts'.[22] Larkin's ideas about modernism are most clearly set out in the introduction to his collection of jazz record reviews. He broadens his discussion of the saxophonist Charlie Parker into general remarks on modernist art:

> To say I don't like modern jazz because it's modernist art simply raises the question of why I don't like modernist art . . . as long as it was only Parker I didn't like, I might believe that my ears had shut up about the age of 25 and that jazz had left me behind. My dislike of Pound and Picasso, both of whom predate me by a considerable margin, can't be explained in this way. The same can be said of Henry Moore and James Joyce (a textbook case of declension from talent to absurdity).

[19] Seamus Heaney, 'Now and in England', *Critical Inquiry*, 3 (Spring 1977), pp. 484–6.
[20] John Press, 'The Poetry of Philip Larkin', *Southern Review* (Louisiana), 13 (1977), p. 132.
[21] Robert Lowell, 'Digressions from Larkin's Twentieth-Century Verse', *Encounter*, 40 (May 1973), p. 68.
[22] Philip Larkin, 'It could only happen in England', *Cornhill Magazine*, 1069 (Autumn 1971), pp. 26, 34, 35.

No, I dislike such things not because they are new, but because they are irresponsible exploitations of technique in contradiction of human life as we know it. This is my essential criticism of modernism, whether perpetrated by Parker, Pound or Picasso: it helps us neither to enjoy nor endure. It will divert us as long as we are prepared to be mystified or outraged, but maintains its hold only by being more mystifying and more outrageous: it has no lasting power.[23]

Against what he sees as the ephemeral exploitation of technique, Larkin champions 'life as we know it' and (a little later in the passage) 'human values'. The moral basis of Larkin's criticism of modernist art, that 'it helps us neither to enjoy nor endure', is rooted in the Augustan ideal of holding a mirror up to nature and saying plainly and unflinchingly what it reflects. The phrase recalls Johnson's Imlac, who tells Rasselas that 'Human life is everywhere a state in which much is to be endured, and little to be enjoyed', and its application to the canons of art echoes Goldsmith's Dr Primrose, who told his daughter that 'books were sweet unreproaching companions to the miserable, and that, if they could not bring us to enjoy life, they would at least teach us to endure it'.[24] This is not to claim that Larkin is a late Augustan in disguise, but the expression of his anti-modernism in such terms at least hints that he shares some of the artistic ideals cherished in the eighteenth century by men such as Johnson and Goldsmith. His determination not to be obscure, his concern with common human feelings and failings, his refusal to strike attitudes, his detachment, his earnest desire not to exclude his reader, all suggest that some features of Larkin's manner are derived from eighteenth-century attitudes. We shall return to this point.

Larkin's anti-modernism was fostered by his reading of Hardy's poetry; for this experience established his confidence in the validity of poetry that was direct and straightforward rather than learned and allusive. Larkin has said: 'When I came to Hardy it was with the sense of relief that I didn't have to try to jack myself up to a concept of poetry that lay outside my own life'.[25] We should discount any notion of influence here, for as Larkin goes on to say, Hardy was more important to him as a kindred poetic spirit than as a formal master: 'Hardy taught one to feel rather than to write—of course one has to use one's own language and

[23] Philip Larkin, *All What Jazz: A Record Diary 1961–68*, Faber and Faber, London 1970, pp. 16–17.

[24] Johnson, *Rasselas*, ch. xi; Goldsmith, *The Vicar of Wakefield*, ch. xxii.

[25] 'Philip Larkin praises the poetry of Thomas Hardy', *The Listener*, 80 (July–December 1968), p. 111.

one's own jargon and one's own situations—and he taught one as well to have confidence in what one felt'.[26] Occasionally one finds in Larkin's poetry a word, usually quaint or archaic, that one may find also in Hardy, but for the most part the significance of Hardy to Larkin was a matter of giving him confidence in himself and his personal feelings as subject-matter for poetry. Hardy has therefore been more important to Larkin's sense of himself than he need be to our sense of Larkin. Hardy may have helped to form Larkin's sensibility, but the later poet's style is all his own. With Hardy as the tutor of his emotions, therefore—Hardy's poetry having been largely ignored because literary criticism, operating under the baleful influence of modernism, 'thrives on the difficult'[27]—Larkin can confidently say that he shares 'no belief in "tradition" or a common myth-kitty or casual allusions in poems to other poems or poets'.[28] And Larkin has justified his own practice on the grounds that it 'cuts out obscurity, it cuts out references to literature and mythology which you cannot be sure [readers starting from cold] may know. It means you are writing fairly simply in the language of ordinary people, using the accepted sense of words and using the accepted grammatical constructions'.[29]

There may well be something disingenuous in all this. For one thing, David Timms has marshalled impressive evidence from Larkin's own pen to suggest that his approach to literature is less anti-intellectual than he would have us believe.[30] For another, the phrase 'the language of ordinary people' blandly disregards the many problems that Wordsworth encountered when he started talking about 'the real language of men'. Just who is an ordinary person? A university librarian? A lighthouse keeper? And would his language include words such as 'lambent' or 'supine'? Larkin simply ignores such questions. Furthermore, Larkin's poems do contain references to other literature: to Gray's 'Elegy', for example, in 'For Sidney Bechet'; to Prospero's famous speech in the fourth act of *The Tempest* in 'Toads'; to E. M. Forster, St Paul's first Epistle to the Corinthians, and the classical name for the south wind in 'Naturally the Foundation will Bear Your Expenses'; and to Tennyson's *The Princess* in 'Lines on a Young Lady's Photograph Album'. In

---

[26] Ibid, p. 111. See also Larkin's introduction to *The North Ship*, p. 10.

[27] Philip Larkin, 'Wanted: Good Hardy Critic', *Critical Quarterly*, 8 (1966), p. 174.

[28] This comment, in *Poets of the 1950s* (p. 78), was not intended for publication when Larkin sent it to the editor.

[29] Interview with Raymond Gardner, *The Guardian*, 31 March 1973, p. 12.

[30] David Timms, *Philip Larkin*, Oliver and Boyd, Edinburgh 1973, pp. 59–68.

addition, the titles of 'I Remember, I Remember' and 'This Be The Verse' allude to poems by Thomas Hood and Robert Louis Stevenson respectively. With the exception of the Tennyson reference none of these is particularly elusive, but they do exist, and their existence rather questions Larkin's professed refusal to do this kind of thing. Furthermore, Larkin's diatribes against modernism contain few references to Yeats, surely a central figure in the development of modernist literature, and certainly a poet with whom Larkin has greater *stylistic* affinity than with Hardy. Thus, while Larkin's attitude to human existence is indubitably more reminiscent of Hardy than of Yeats, his impressive organization of the large stanza and his fine sense of metrical arrangement may owe a good deal to Yeats; and Edna Longley has pointed to his 'Yeats-like capacity to endow the polysyllabic abstractions with sensuous texture by means of subtle assonances and giving their strongest stresses maximum opportunity within the line'.[31] It is at least possible that Larkin has assimilated more from Yeats than he is aware of, and that his dismissal of Yeats (in his introduction to *The North Ship*) as a youthful infatuation should be taken with a grain of salt.

It is of course impossible for any writer wholly to escape the influence of modernism by trying to write as though it never happened, and there are two further aspects of Larkin's writing which place question-marks against his disparagement of modernist art's over-exploitation of technique. Their nature is such that they are almost impossible to discuss outside the context of particular poems, but they must be mentioned here. The first of these concerns the presentation of the poem to the reader's eye. Larkin never forgets that the act of reading a poem is itself part of that poem's action, and thus the complexity of a poem's coherence on the page is frequently used to stimulate our perception of the poem's thematic meaning. This aspect of Larkin's work has been almost ignored. He has become adept at exploiting such things as typographical variation, the fact that rhymes are sometimes seen rather than heard, and the visual organization of line-ending and stanza-arrangement. Such technical features may function in a poem as mimetic puns or enactments of its statement, and these kinds of visual wit can also give the reader hints about his likely reception of or relationship to what the poem says. It would be misleading to suggest that these things are peculiar to modernism, but the visual organization of a written work of art as an

---

[31] Edna Longley, 'Larkin, Edward Thomas and the Tradition', Philip Larkin issue of *Phoenix*, p. 84. Longley also claims that 'Above all, Larkin shares with Yeats an adjectival habit' (p. 85).

essential aspect of its total meaning has been fiercely adopted by modernist writers; and such devices, although he may use them less dramatically than Joyce, are central to much of Larkin's poetry. Of course the notion of expressive form is as applicable to *Tom Jones* as it is to *Ulysses*, but the visual nature of Joyce's formal development in *Ulysses* gives him more in common with Larkin than the poet may care to admit. Larkin's own statements do tend to obscure the necessary relationship of technique and content in any work of art,[32] but they particularly tempt us to overlook it in his own poetry. The other feature of Larkin's work that bears directly on modernist technique is his use of a *persona*, speaker, or mask. As Pinsky has said: 'the use of a borrowed voice or alter-identity, as speaker or central character partly distinct from the poet, constitutes one of the most widely noted, perhaps over-emphasized, critically chewed, and fundamental aspects of modernism'.[33] Larkin's much admired exploitation of the tones of the speaking voice implies a speaking presence which lends itself to vastly different uses, and while this again is by no means peculiar to modernism it is nevertheless a central feature of modernist literature. The critical geography here has been most thoroughly charted by Robert Langbaum, who has pointed out that the breakdown of the early Romantic belief in the integrity of the self as it occurred in the nineteenth century not only gave rise to the dramatic monologue as a form in which 'the poet gives lyric utterance to a character who is identified as completely as possible as not himself';[34] it led also to the proliferation of masks and *personae* through which modern literature dramatically enacts its concern with the problem of human identity. Thus Larkin's frequent exploitation of a speaker puts him closer to the mainstream of modernism than he has himself been prepared to recognize: the speaker of 'Vers de Société', for example, is surely a

---

[32] See, for example, Larkin's interview with Ian Hamilton in *The London Magazine*, 4 (November 1964), reprinted in Graham Martin and P. N. Furbank (eds), *Twentieth Century Poetry: Critical Essays and Documents*, The Open University Press, Milton Keynes 1975. Subsequent page references to this interview will be to the latter.

[33] Pinsky, *The Situation of Poetry*, p. 14.

[34] Robert Langbaum, 'The Mysteries of Identity: A Theme in Modern Literature', *The Modern Spirit: Essays on the Continuity of Nineteenth and Twentieth Century Literature*, Chatto and Windus, London 1970, p. 168. This essay states Langbaum's ideas in their most compact form. Originally published in *The American Scholar* in 1965, it is a development of some ideas in his book *The Poetry of Experience. The Dramatic Monologue in Modern Literary Tradition* (1957), and an anticipation of his recent study of modern literature, *The Mysteries of Identity* (1977).

descendant of J. Alfred Prufrock; and it is fair to say that Larkin's speakers and their various effects have hardly been scrutinized. Kuby's observation that 'I' in any given poem 'is not necessarily the poet'[35] comes too late in her study to be of much use, and receives little expansion. Martin Scofield has claimed that 'the personality of the speaker . . . is an integral part of the poetic effect'[36] of most poems, and Alan Brownjohn tells us that there have been 'some notable misunderstandings of [Larkin's] intention where he has adopted a *persona*',[37] but neither of these statements is applied or substantiated. Most helpfully, Christopher Ricks has suggested that 'the best of Larkin lives in the context of an imagined life',[38] but not enough attention has been paid generally to the means by which lives are imagined.

Most criticism has failed to progress beyond the recognition that Larkin at times uses a speaker. On the assumption that a speaker is always a means to an end, I have examined the manifold uses to which Larkin puts his speakers, and the various effects of those uses. I am generally indebted here to R. W. Rader's article, 'The Dramatic Monologue and Related Literary Forms',[39] which takes Robert Langbaum's distinction (in *The Poetry of Experience*) between the dramatic lyric and the dramatic monologue as the starting-point for an extended discussion of the relationship between author and speaker in poems which employ an 'I'. It must be stressed, however, that this debt is general: Rader never mentions Larkin, and I have used neither his terminology nor his categories; for many of Larkin's poems do not use an 'I', and any consideration of masks, speakers or *personae*, leads inevitably to the broader issue of the author's relationship with his reader. A speaker is a means, but only one means, of engaging the reader. In some poems which do not have an 'I' the tone may still be 'as unpressingly intimate as the touch of a hand on one's arm',[40] and in looking at Larkin's creation of such intimacy it is necessary to go beyond the dramatic use of a speaker to examine the other ways in which an authorial presence is established.

[35] Kuby, *An Uncommon Poet*, p. 137.
[36] Martin Scofield, 'The Poetry of Philip Larkin', *Massachusetts Review*, 17 (1976), p. 380.
[37] Alan Brownjohn, *Philip Larkin*, Writers and Their Work no. 247, Longmans, Harlow 1975, p. 13.
[38] Christopher Ricks, 'The words and music of life', *Sunday Times*, 7 January 1968, p. 39.
[39] R. W. Rader, 'The Dramatic Monologue and Related Literary Forms', *Critical Inquiry*, 3 (Autumn 1976).
[40] Calvin Bedient, 'Philip Larkin' in *Eight Contemporary Poets*, Oxford University Press, London 1974, p. 77.

This is not to claim that Larkin is a modernist in disguise. But to lump him with the English 'movement' of the 'fifties as a poet writing about ordinary life and ordinary people in ordinary language is to imply a very ordinary poet and elicit an uncritical yawn. It may well be, as Seamus Heaney has said, that Larkin looks into England rather than up to it,[41] but what does he find there, and what has he done with it poetically? Furthermore, Larkin's comments on his art have been so self-effacing that his own technique and method have not received the close and sustained examination they deserve. It is not enough for Geoffrey Thurley to assure us blandly that Larkin's poetry is 'easy and lissom in gait' or that he is 'rarely hard-up for a rhyme'.[42] Such superficial condescension is less than helpful, for as John Wain has rightly stressed 'Larkin's rhymes are a study in themselves',[43] although this study has yet to be undertaken. So offhand have been Larkin's remarks about his own work that he tends to give 'an overwhelming impression of not much caring for the business at all',[44] but such hints as he has given have been generally overlooked. His comment on the necessity he feels for the use of rhyme and metre has inspired proper examination of neither his rhymes nor his metrics, any more than his revealing comment on the self-dramatizing element in poetry has inspired any penetrating glances at his *personae*.[45] What follows in these pages is an attempt to examine in detail the significant major features of Larkin's poetry. The main aim is to illuminate by analysis the subtlety and sophistication of the techniques whereby the poetry achieves its peculiarly distinctive flavour: the poet's various uses of a speaker, his own submergence in a poem's technique, his idiosyncratic exploitation of rhyme, syntax and stanza-form, his constant appeal to the visual sense (including the act of reading), his tendency to move his poems towards general statements. The chapters have been structured around the chronology of Larkin's work, in the hope that a sense of development may emerge from the discussion.

There are of course other extended discussions of Larkin's work, and in some ways my approach has been anticipated by David Timms' volume in the 'Modern Writers' series, *Philip Larkin*.[46] Timms avoids many of the

[41] Heaney, 'Now and in England', p. 488.
[42] Geoffrey Thurley, *The Ironic Harvest: English Poetry in the Twentieth Century*, Edward Arnold, London 1974, p. 142.
[43] John Wain, 'The Poetry of Philip Larkin', *Malahat Review*, 39 (1976), p. 104.
[44] Interview with Raymond Gardner, *The Guardian*, 31 March 1973, p. 12.
[45] Both these comments are to be found in Larkin's interview with Ian Hamilton in Martin and Furbank (eds), *Twentieth Century Poetry*, pp. 245, 246.
[46] For full reference, see n. 30, above.

pitfalls I have indicated. He recognizes the frequent existence of a speaker who cannot automatically be identified with the poet, he makes occasionally penetrating remarks on rhyme and metre, and he gives an excellent account of Larkin's relationship to the 'movement'. Anyone writing on Larkin must do so with Timms' book in mind. However, the overall emphases of this study fall somewhat differently from his own. Our discussions do overlap occasionally, generally in relation to particular poems; but at times we disagree, and at other times I have tried either to emphasize such features of the poems as Timms has chosen not to discuss, or to elaborate on his insights. Lolette Kuby's *An Uncommon Poet for the Common Man*, which has also been mentioned, suffers from a persistent tendency to paraphrase Larkin's poems in philosophical jargon. To describe 'Absences' as 'the verbalization of . . . a negative mystical experience, into the ineffable Nothing' (p. 55) is to get perilously close to an ineffable nothing, and a chapter title such as 'The Limitation and Implementation of Free Will' (ch. 3) does not augur well for a close look at the poetry. Kuby's assertion that 'the meaning of time in his poems extends to complex metaphysical concepts involving the role that time plays in human dualism and the disconnection of reality and ideality' (p. 77) is likewise symptomatic of her tendency to abstract metaphysics from the poetry. The strength of Roger Day's Open University study[47] is that it does concern itself with specifics and never gets far from particular poems. But its limited length reduces Larkin to only a handful of poems, however judiciously chosen, and its layout in systematically numbered paragraphs and sub-sections, however enhancing to its effectiveness as a teaching aid, drastically disrupts its continuity. Much of the best criticism exists in reviews and articles, especially the reviews (mentioned above) of *The Whitsun Weddings* and *High Windows* by Christopher Ricks and John Bayley respectively. And while J. R. Watson may overstate his case in claiming that 'Larkin's poetry celebrates the unexpressed, deeply felt longings for sacred time and sacred space',[48] his aptly-titled 'The Other Larkin' represents a salutary shift of emphasis away from what Charles Tomlinson deplored as 'the suburban mental ratio'[49] of the middlebrow muse. Less directly, and whether or not Larkin accepted Donald Davie's *Purity of Diction in English Verse*[50] as the prescriptive 'manifesto' its author considered it to be, this book is helpful to an understanding of the

[47] Roger Day, *Philip Larkin*, The Open University Press, Milton Keynes 1976.
[48] Watson, 'The Other Larkin', p. 354.
[49] Tomlinson, 'The Middlebrow Muse', p. 215.
[50] Donald Davie, *Purity of Diction in English Verse*, 1952, reprinted Routledge and Kegan Paul, London 1967, p. 197.

demands that Larkin's kind of poetry makes of the reader, especially in what Davie has to say about metaphorical restraint, the power of verbs, and 'the tang of common usage'. Some of these, and others, are mentioned in the notes.

The charge most persistently levelled against Larkin's poetry is that his capability is applied in almost entirely negative ways. M. L. Rosenthal has complained about his 'fundamental lugubriousness',[51] and J. M. Newton, reviewing *The Whitsun Weddings*, laments Larkin's lack of nobility : 'there is no sense of a delicate, generous spirit struggling against defeat, let alone of a strong one'.[52] In all probability Larkin would regard such a noble struggle as yet another example of futile human posturing, and in any case he has bluntly stated his opinion that 'there is not much pleasure to be got from the truth about things as anyone sees it'.[53] This statement points us again to Larkin's sense of his temperamental affinity with Hardy, who shared a similarly bleak view of human experience, and who was just as annoyed by charges of pessimism as Larkin has been. Defending Hardy, and indeed echoing Hardy's own General Preface to the 1912 Wessex Edition of his novels, Larkin has insisted that 'the presence of pain in Hardy's novels is a positive, not a negative quality—not the mechanical working out of some pre-determined allegiance to pessimism or any other concept, but the continual and imaginative celebration of what is both the truest and most important element in life, most important in the sense of most necessary to spiritual development'.[54] As we learn from 'Deceptions', suffering is exact. Moreover, what Larkin sees as the central focus of Hardy's emotional life—the paradox that Hardy could not write his love poetry for his first wife until after she had died, when it had to come 'with a flood of regret and remorse for what he had lost'—is evidence of the truth that there is 'an inevitable bias in life towards unhappiness'.[55] We may still feel that Larkin fails to answer adequately the accusations of negativism, and it is as well to recognize that some poems, early ones for the most part, are concentrated too exclusively on the point at which self-pity becomes self-loathing. That this tendency has gradually been exorcized from the

[51] M. L. Rosenthal, *The New Poets: American and British Poetry Since World War II*, Oxford University Press, New York 1967, p. 234.

[52] J. M. Newton, ' . . . And a More Comprehensive Soul', *Cambridge Quarterly*, 1 (1965–6), p. 98. K. M. Sagar's response, and Newton's reply to that, are to be found on pp. 178–82 of this same journal.

[53] Philip Larkin, 'Context', *The London Magazine*, Vol. 1, No. 11 (February 1962), p. 32.

[54] Larkin, 'Wanted: Good Hardy Critic', p. 178.

[55] Philip Larkin, 'Mrs. Hardy's memories', *Critical Quarterly*, 4 (1962), p. 79.

poetry is the result of two combined factors: first, Larkin has developed various means of distancing himself from the feelings presented in the poems; and second, his poetry manifests a growing recognition of the power of ritual as an ordering process in human affairs generally. Although Larkin lacks the later Yeats's resounding and energetic confidence in human positives, his poetry is surely not without its affirmations, however carefully they may be qualified. He finds value in the things men do in common out of instinctive impulses, and his own detached perspective enables him to comment on the significance of such things as going to the seaside, or to the annual show. The effect is of humanity surviving in spite of itself, of the individual life vindicated by the experience of the race. Such a perception may not be new, but it is hardly shallow or complacent, and it does represent a positive focus. Equally important, Larkin sees the very act of writing as creatively affirmative; it is 'in some form or other, compensation, assertion of oneself in an indifferent or hostile environment, demonstration (by writing about it) that one is in command of a situation'.[56] To articulate and order one's perceptions of experience, whatever their nature, suggests a form of control over them, and as such represents a positive action.

The unavoidable fact, however, is that the major impact of Larkin's poetry comes from the power with which it reminds us of the snares, ambushes and pitfalls which the imagination is all too often preparing for us. For Larkin, as for Johnson's Imlac, the motivating forces of human behaviour are sadly destructive ones, stemming from 'that hunger of imagination which preys incessantly upon life' and 'the insufficiency of human enjoyments'.[57] The opening of Johnson's 'On the Death of Dr Robert Levet' provides a valid analogy:

> Condemn'd to hope's delusive mine,
> As on we toil from day to day,
> By sudden blasts, or slow decline,
> Our social comforts drop away.

The central metaphor gives us a situation of unmitigated pessimism: condemned by the human condition to spend our lives digging in the delusive mine of hope, the harder we work the worse our situation is doomed to become. The more we hope the more we destroy, and the deeper we entrench ourselves. Without the consolation of religion (an option open to Johnson in a way that it is not to Larkin) this poem would collapse. The vanity of human wishes may not be an 'optimistic' theme,

[56] Larkin, 'Context', p. 32.
[57] *Rasselas*, ch. xxxii.

but its centrality is undeniable, and Larkin's derivation of so much poetic strength from it affirms the human centrality of his own poetry. It is surely fair to invoke the authority of Hardy's General Preface here:

> Existence is either ordered in a certain way, or it is not so ordered, and conjectures which harmonize best with experience are removed above all comparison with other conjectures which do not so harmonize. So that to say one view is worse than other views without proving it erroneous implies the possibility of a false view being better or more expedient than a true view; and no pragmatic proppings can make that *idolum specus* stand on its feet, for it postulates a prescience denied to humanity.

Both Hardy and Johnson make it hard to disagree with their points of view. Furthermore, Johnson's poem opens with an appeal to common experience—'we toil' and 'our social comforts'—and then lights on the particular example of Levet, only to drift inevitably back to the area of generalization. If Johnson's poem begins with a generalization, Larkin's poems frequently end in such a manner; and this question of generalization raises another critical problem which again has been most forcefully put by J. M. Newton, who says that Larkin may sometimes 'be asking the reader to take slowly and solemnly lines that either immediately or after reflection prove to be banal'.[58] Sometimes this is true. When we are told at the end of 'Dockery and Son' that life passes whether or not we use it, we are merely being reminded of a truism. But the first part of this poem's closing statement—'Life is first boredom, then fear'—may invite disagreement, and if this is so then our response to the rest of the concluding generalization is likely to be more complex than simple acceptance. Paradoxically it is only possible to talk about the effectiveness or otherwise of generalization by examining the particular context in which it occurs, and in the case of 'Dockery and Son' the generalization has grown out of a long meditation: it cannot be detached and pointed to as a moral, but must be viewed as a part of the poem's totality. And the general point here is that we should always see the generalizations of Larkin's poetry in relation to what has preceded them in the poem, and try to establish how they are affected by their poetic context. The end of 'Dockery and Son' is hard to wriggle away from precisely because it is offered as part, albeit the culminating part, of the poem; but that we should be left questioning or ambivalent about what may sound banal is surely part of the poet's strategy. At other times, too, Larkin may either present us with generalizations that are patently

[58] Newton, '. . . And a More Comprehensive Soul', p. 182.

suspect, or that are so heavily qualified as to demand a questioning response. They neither have nor are supposed to have the authority with which Dr Johnson undoubtedly wished to invest his own generalizations.

David Holbrook has taken marked exception both to the generalizing habit, 'which stands in the place of exactness, or of any focus on defined feeling',[59] and also to Larkin's detachment. These two things are different sides of the same coin which, for Holbrook, is not legal poetic tender. His discussion of 'The Whitsun Weddings' uses such words as 'cruelty' and 'hostility' to describe the attitude of the speaker; he manipulates the speaker's detachment into a class distance by placing him in a first-class railway compartment; and he thinks the poem both expresses and fosters a 'hatred of human beings'.[60] Holbrook can only turn his dislike of this detached manner into an attack on the speaker's 'derogatory attitude' by a particularly wilful misreading of the poem; and while there are critics who invest so heavily in Larkin that they cannot bring themselves to admit that he is capable of writing a bad poem (John Wain is a case in point), Holbrook's polarization of his own poetic ideal against the reality of Larkin's poetry is no more than an example of an opposite tendency.

For we cannot demand Romanticism of all our poets, although like the writer of the article quoted at the beginning of this introduction, Holbrook seems to lament the absence of the esemplastic power of the imagination from contemporary English poetry. It is possible to label Larkin broadly as anti-romantic, if we take that term to refer to the distrust of the imagination which informs all his work; although it is not unfair to point out that Samuel Taylor Coleridge, to whom we are largely indebted for the Romantic theory of the imagination, would find himself very much at home in the world of Larkin's poems, haunted as he was for so much of his life by thoughts of unfulfilled promise, by the dread of failure, and by the discrepancy in his own life between ideas and their realization. In any case, against Holbrook's disappointment at this poem's failure to provide 'something transcendent' should be set James Naremore's confident description of 'The Whitsun Weddings' as an 'epiphany', and John Bayley's recognition of 'epiphanic intermissions' in the poems generally.[61] Indeed, for just about every critical statement on Larkin one can find an anti-statement. Thus, whereas Anthony Thwaite

---

[59] Holbrook, *Lost Bearings in English Poetry*, p. 165.
[60] Ibid., pp. 167–8. Holbrook's objections to the end of the poem fail to take account of the qualifications with which Larkin surrounds the energy and fruition: see Bedient, *Eight Contemporary Poets*, p. 93.
[61] James Naremore, 'Philip Larkin's "Lost World"', *Contemporary Literature*,

believes that his themes are 'unshakably major', Clive James thinks 'It ought to be obvious that Larkin is not a universal poet in the thematic sense'.[62] Whereas Christopher Ricks believes that Larkin starts with a Wordsworthian subject, Calvin Bedient contrasts his whole approach with Wordsworth's view of the calling.[63] To James, again, 'Larkin is the poet of the void. The one affirmation his work offers is the possibility that when we have lost everything else the problem of beauty will still remain'; while Alan Brownjohn, in stark contrast, celebrates 'a poetry which catches and makes beautiful the stuff of the experience of common men in the twentieth century'.[64] Any poet capable of inspiring such divergent, even contradictory responses, is worthy of detailed critical attention.

In bringing that attention to bear on the poetry we should above all bear in mind Philip Gardner's exhortation to 'see Larkin's work in a wider perspective than that provided by the poetical fashions of the fifties'.[65] Any impression given in the preceding pages that Larkin is either a closet modernist or a displaced Augustan will doubtless be shattered by a glance at the poetry. The purpose of this introduction, however, has been to raise the complex of critical issues surrounding the poetry, and in doing this it has been necessary to point to the many traditions that have shaped and nurtured the work of this most unassuming poet. For the moment, however, we need recall only Larkin's stated conviction 'that the reader's first encounter with the poem must be a silent, active one, an absorption of spelling and stanza-arrangement as much as paraphrasable meaning and corrective historical knowledge'.[66] It is hoped that the following pages will further both the challenge and the enjoyment of such close encounters of the first and subsequent kinds.

15 (1974), p. 342; and John Bayley, 'Too Good for This World', p. 653. It is of course supremely ironical that a term which entered criticism *via* Joyce's aesthetic theory should be applied in positive and laudatory terms to a poet who has set himself against modernism and all it stands for—a fact which should inspire further thoughts about the nature of Larkin's relationship to modernism.

[62] Anthony Thwaite, 'The Poetry of Philip Larkin' in Martin Dodsworth (ed.), *The Survival of Poetry*, Faber and Faber, London 1970, p. 54; Clive James, 'Wolves of Memory', *Encounter*, 42 (June 1974), p. 66.

[63] Ricks, 'The Whitsun Weddings', p. 7; Bedient, *Eight Contemporary Poets*, p. 69.

[64] James, 'Wolves of Memory', p. 71; Brownjohn, *Philip Larkin*, p. 32.

[65] Philip Gardner, 'The Wintry Drum', Larkin issue of *Phoenix*, 27–40; p 32. This article was reprinted from *Dalhousie Review*, 48 (1968).

[66] Philip Larkin, 'Masters' Voices', *New Statesman*, 63 (January–June 1962), p. 170.

I

Early Work

Larkin began to acquire a substantial reputation as a poet following the publication of *The Less Deceived* in 1955. By this time he was thirty-three and had been writing and publishing for over ten years, but *The Less Deceived* is rightly regarded as the first mature fruit of Larkin's writing. This volume itself incorporated work from two pamphlets which had appeared in 1951 and 1955, and which had been preceded by two novels, published in 1946 and 1947, and a single volume of poems, *The North Ship*, published in 1945. Since *The Less Deceived*, Larkin has produced a slender collection of poems approximately every ten years. There is thus a sense in which the decade from 1945 to 1955 may be regarded as Larkin's most productive period, and although the writing it produced is certainly not his best, it is nevertheless interesting and important to the student of his poetry. For the pattern of this decade—a book of poems quickly followed by two novels, then a return to poetry and the eventual publication of another volume of poems—suggests a journey of experimentation. Such a journey is undertaken by most writers; and in Larkin's case, as in the case of many others, the goal of the journey was the outgrowing of youthful influences and the discovery of a distinctive and individual manner.

However typical this pattern of experimentation may be, the striking thing about it here is the short burst of novel writing, which quickly produced two books and which was then abandoned once and for all. Many of the writers we think of primarily as poets have written novels, and vice versa, and it is natural to assume that a writer's work in one genre may illuminate his or her work in another. But the astonishing advances between *The North Ship* and *The Less Deceived* suggest that Larkin's novels were of particular significance to his development as a poet, and indeed any account of Larkin's early work must pay close attention to them for what they can tell us about his efforts to find himself as a writer. After glancing briefly at *The North Ship*, therefore, this chapter will attempt to assess the importance to Larkin's career of *Jill* and *A Girl in Winter*.

It is impossible to read the juvenilia of any writer without trying, with all the benefit of hindsight, to trace the development of themes and concerns that seem to have been present from the first. Apart from the occasional hint, however, it is difficult to find much promise of things to come in *The North Ship*. It hardly foreshadows, in any significant sense, either the interests or the methods of Larkin's later work. Too much of the poetry is derivative—only rarely does it rise much above pastiche; and while some poems do express moods of disappointment or isolation (both of which are central to the later and more mature work), the moods here tend to be insubstantial and 'literary' in the worst sense. The words fail to convince that the feelings are real. Larkin's own retrospective (1966) introduction to the reissue of *The North Ship* makes no bones about the limitations of the poetry. He traces them to his own lack of poetic identity at the time, and he talks also of the several abandoned selves he recognizes in the poems: the ex-schoolboy, the undergraduate, and the 'immediately post-Oxford' self, with their respective mentors of Auden, Dylan Thomas, and Yeats. And he observes, in a way that is typically both honest and self-deprecating: 'This search for a style was merely one aspect of a general immaturity' (p. 8).

The Yeats he mentions, for example, is predominantly the immature Yeats, the Yeats of the Celtic twilight; and Larkin confesses that he tried to write like Yeats 'not because I liked his personality or understood his ideas, but out of infatuation with his music' (p. 9). The majority of the poems in *The North Ship* hover in an atmosphere of vague romanticism recalling the worst excesses of the Pre-Raphaelite movement. Drifting aimlessly in a dreamworld from which the pressure of personal feeling is almost wholly absent, the poetry lacks concrete focus:

> There were no mouths
> To drink of the wind,
> Nor any eyes
> To sharpen on the stars'
> Wide heaven-holding,
> Only the sound
> Long sibilant-muscled trees
> Were lifting up, the black poplars.
>
> And in their blazing solitude
> The stars sang in their sockets through the night:
> "Blow bright, blow bright
> The coal of this unquickened world."
>
> ('Night-Music', p. 23)

19

An attempt to create an emotional landscape manages only to evoke the background to a mood. Worse, the mingling of sense-impressions adds up to very little, as the final clumsy conceit testifies; and the emotion, through being reduced to a trick of style or sleight of association, is revealed as patently bogus.

Everything is impressionistic, and nothing is analysed in any depth:

> To wake, and hear a cock
> Out of the distance crying,
> To pull the curtains back
> And see the clouds flying—
> How strange it is
> For the heart to be loveless, and as cold as these.
>
> ('Dawn', p. 15)

Sense-impressions, particularly visual ones, are used as emotional equivalents, yet because it is impossible to locate an emotion, the poem is no more than ponderous and empty. The clouds may be, or may appear 'cold', but their 'lovelessness' is imposed by the poet, and the reader simply has to accept the imposition. In trying very hard *not* to be subjective (the verbs are nearly all infinitives), the poem goes nowhere. And it is worth comparing this poem with 'Sad Steps' in *High Windows* to see how this kind of emotion needs to be localized within a subjective presence in a concrete situation for its expression to be at all convincing.

The poems are too static. 'Winter' (p. 19) lists a series of correspondences between moods and details in the landscape, but here the comparisons between human and natural are too heavily symbolic: thistles are 'crowded like men', each horse is 'like a passion', and the symbolic significance of the landscape is thus crudely stated by simile rather than established and used. Once again we are left with a series of equations adding up to very little. Some poems are melodramatic without any sense of true drama, populated by cardboard stage-props rather than human figures. At the conclusion of poem xxiv (p. 37), for example, the lovers part

> As two tall ships, wind-mastered, wet with light,
> Break from an estuary with their courses set,
> And waving part, and waving drop from sight.

The full silliness of turning people into ships becomes apparent only when one works back from the terms of the simile to the human parting it describes. The result is ludicrous.

Nevertheless, a closer look at the construction of many of the poems suggests that Larkin has taken great care over them. The technique is nearly always painstaking—so much so, in fact, that the poet seems to be more concerned with rhyme and versification than with actually saying anything. Thus, in the last-mentioned poem the extravagant imagery may easily mask the care taken with rhyme, which works to ensure that the poem, for all its extravagance, does develop. Larkin has used the rhyming pattern of a sonnet (octave and sestet), yet structurally the poem is broken into units of nine and five lines. The break in the poem's movement between the ninth and tenth lines, which is a syntactical as well as a structural break, is therefore bridged by the rhyme, for 'use' at the end of the ninth line is echoed in 'loose' at the end of the eleventh. Rhyme and verse form draw attention to each other in a way that may seem mannered, but it is not sloppy, and it can be explained as an attempt to impose form and structure on poems which are for the most part less than precise. The rhetoric may be empty, but the organization is careful.[1]

Larkin has generally aligned himself with poets to whom content is more important than technique,[2] but the fact is that in these poems he has little to say. The lack of direction is suggested by the lack of titles (only eight poems out of thirty-two are titled); and this is in marked contrast to the later Larkin, who is adept at using titles for sardonic emphasis. There are occasional hints of the mature poet's attitude—it is characteristic of Larkin that he should show us a fairy-tale world through the eyes of the ugly sister[3]—but most of the poems are unmemorable. Larkin's own later acknowledgement of the derivative nature of these poems is an admission that he had little sense of himself as a writer when he composed them. And at times he goes to such lengths to suppress any hint of a tangible subjective presence that he can become unreadable:

> Climbing the hill within the deafening wind
> The blood unfurled itself, was proudly borne
> High over meadows where white horses stood;
> Up the steep woods it echoed like a horn
> Till at the summit under shining trees
> It cried: Submission is the only good;

[1] See also poem xxiii (p. 36): each of the two seven-line stanzas opens with a quatrain and ends with a couplet, the common rhyme in the fifth line of each stanza binding them together; and poem xxix (p. 42), throughout which the first rhyme-word 'youth' echoes insistently until it merges finally with 'death'.

[2] Ian Hamilton interview in Graham Martin and P. N. Furbank (eds), *Twentieth-Century Poetry*, The Open University Press, Milton Keynes 1975, p. 243.

[3] 'Ugly Sister', p. 31.

Let me become an instrument sharply stringed
For all things to strike music as they please.
(poem ix, p. 21)

The syntax of this long sentence is appallingly over-complex. Instead of talking about himself the speaker talks of his blood, or rather *the* blood, as if unwilling to admit to having any feelings. And while the dream-world trappings of white horses and shining trees do not help to dispel the general air of unreality, the extraordinary construction of the sentence is the greatest obstacle to understanding. What is presumably an attempt to raise the experience out of the subjective misfires, and the poem fails to ring true. In the eleventh line an 'I' enters the poem, but it has taken a long time to emerge from 'the blood' and it quickly slips back into 'the heart'. Yet again, however, we can see rhyme being used carefully to bind the stanza-sentence together: 'stringed' in the penultimate line reaches right back to the 'wind' of the opening line, and although the echo may not be quite vibrant enough it does underscore the image of a wind-harp.

It would be superfluous as well as unkind to dwell further on the defects of Larkin's immature work. In any case, the weaknesses are sufficiently shown up by the stronger poems in *The North Ship*, which are characterized by the very thing that the poems discussed above so conspicuously lack: a tangible subjective presence informing and organizing the progression of thought and feeling. The voice of poem xx, 'I see a girl dragged by the wrists' (p. 32) may not be distinctively Larkin's, but the poem carries greater conviction and authority than any of those discussed so far; and the reason for this is that we can chart the poem's development through involvement with the directly speaking 'I'. From the forthrightness of the opening sentence we are presented with an interaction between the speaker and what he sees:

> I see a girl dragged by the wrists
> Across a dazzling field of snow,
> And there is nothing in me that resists.
> Once it would not be so;
> Once I should choke with powerless jealousies;
> But now I seem devoid of subtlety,
> As simple as the things I see,
> Being no more, no less, than two weak eyes.

An internal debate about expectations of human life is dramatically projected on to things seen, and the speaker's own expectations are gradually resolved in terms of his relationship to things outside himself.

The rhyme-scheme is simple and binding without being obtrusive, and the varying line-length easily adapts the regular stanzaic form of the poem through its movement of realization ('For the first time I'm content to see . . .'), question ('Else how should two old ragged men . . .'), and expostulation ('Damn all explanatory rhymes!').

Of course the speaker sees projections of himself, in the girl whose zest he would emulate, and in the two old ragged men who show him what he must be and do by acquiescing in their lot rather than struggling against it. Even if there is still too much Yeats in the poem, and even if the wish-fulfilling conclusion makes the poem end in retreat, it is nevertheless gratifying to be made aware of a thinking mind in the process of formulating its response to experience. And at the same time as the visualized scenes in the poem provide a meaningful focus for the speaker's meditation, they have enough detail to convince us that they are naturalistic. A more complex and concentrated meditation, in poem xxx (p. 43), is not permitted the luxury of a fantasy ending:

> Summer broke and drained. Now we are safe.
> The days lose confidence, and can be faced
> Indoors. This is your last, meticulous hour,
> Cut, gummed; pastime of a provincial winter.

The poem is less about the girl, the 'you' of the poem, than it is about the 'I', the attitude of the speaker. He says little directly about himself—'I slept' and 'I dare not think [you] alive'; and the only point of grammatical identification between speaker and girl—'Now *we* are safe'—is, as the context reveals, chillingly defensive in its notion of safety.

The girl has ceased to exist as a human being and survives only as an image, a name, or a belief 'Long since embedded in the static past'. The idea of stasis is central. 'Severed' and 'wing-stiff' conjure the image of a dead insect pinned out in a collector's case, and anticipate the de-humanizing activity of sticking photographs in an album, with which the poem concludes. The girl may as well be dead, for she lives in the speaker's mind only as an image. There is a kind of security in having her 'cut' and 'gummed' to the page, turned into an image freed from the demands of time and process which are all too liable to bring disappointment. The final phrase, 'pastime of a provincial winter', wryly acknowledges the futility of such an attempt to compensate for the fulfilment which the relationship presumably failed to provide. There is also a suggestion, in the syntactical organization and progression of the two short sentences in the eleventh line, that 'broke' and 'drained' are transitive verbs with 'us' as the object implied by the speaker, but with 'me' as the object understood by the reader. It is clear that the speaker 'dare not' think the girl alive, because to do so would threaten the equanimity of his self-deceptive security. This amounts psychologically to murder; for he has reduced her to a memory preserved in physical form.

Larkin has said: 'I think the impulse to preserve lies at the bottom of all art';[4] and his own art frequently expresses the desire of the human heart to cling to aspects of experience which are incapable of preservation. Such a desire may well be impossible to realize, but it is surely authentic, and of course the very impossibility lends great emotional tension to the desire. Furthermore the poem's dramatic element grows out of this tension, for this speaker's 'impulse to preserve' is not unlike that expressed by Porphyria's lover in Browning's poem. Yet whereas Browning's strategy is to shock us into recognition of the pathological condition of his speaker, the drama of Larkin's poem is more subdued. Both speakers express the attraction of similar and suspect psychological states, yet we reject Porphyria's lover as a psychopathic killer while the more muted nature of Larkin's poem leaves us questioning and uncertain. This manner is developed in later poetry.

The final poem in the 1966 reissue of *The North Ship* (poem xxxii, p. 48) was not included in the original collection. Written about a year later than the other poems, it also is concerned with the preservation of a moment and a feeling, although it has a directness and an honest perplexity not to be found elsewhere in the book. With both wonder and surprise the speaker celebrates a spontaneous emotion, yet questions any idea of love as capable of preservation. The reality of the question is established by the immediacy with which the speaker's feelings emerge from the scene, and the opening participial phrase introduces one of Larkin's favourite ways of beginning a poem:[5]

> Waiting for breakfast, while she brushed her hair,
> I looked down at the empty hotel yard
> Once meant for coaches. Cobblestones were wet,
> But sent no light back to the loaded sky,
> Sunk as it was with mist down to the roofs.
> Drainpipes and fire-escape climbed up

[4] Quoted in D. J. Enright (ed.), *Poets of the 1950s*, The Kenkyusha Press, Tokyo 1955, p. 77.
[5] See, for example: 'Maiden Name', 'I Remember, I Remember' (*The Less Deceived*); 'Here', 'Toads Revisited', 'Naturally the Foundation will Bear Your Expenses', 'Talking in Bed', 'Send No Money' (*The Whitsun Weddings*); 'Forget What Did', 'Sad Steps' (*High Windows*).

Past rooms still burning their electric light:
I thought: Featureless morning, featureless night.

The verbal movement from 'I looked' to 'I thought' enacts the poem's overall movement: the scene gives rise to certain thoughts which are then belied by the reality of human feelings. As the poem develops the particularized visual details of this opening stanza are modified, becoming semi-naturalistic in the second stanza and disappearing altogether in the third. The movement to abstraction is firmly governed by the detail of the opening, however, with the result that the poem remains tangible, and that its tangibilty is achieved in irregular form and with hardly any rhyme suggests again that technique has been standing in for substance in many poems in *The North Ship*. None of these three last-mentioned poems is a masterpiece, yet in their different ways they are marked advances on the rest of the collection. They present us with thinking minds whose fluxes and refluxes are more engaging than the static passivity of most of the poems; they develop dramatically; and as they question the permanence of human emotion they also probe various kinds of illusion. In fact they ring in the major concerns of Larkin's novels, to which we should now turn.

The title of Larkin's first novel, *Jill*, is somewhat misleading, for the book is far less concerned with the girl of the title than it is with the working-class protagonist John Kemp and his experiences during his first term at Oxford University in 1940. Larkin is interested not so much in what John does as in what he thinks and feels, so that the author's imagination is engaged primarily with the imagination of the central character. Furthermore, the fact that John is working-class is arguably more central to the novel than Larkin has been prepared to admit. In his 1963 introduction to the novel Larkin said, in response to an American critic who recognized in John 'the displaced working-class hero': 'My hero's background, though an integral part of the story, was not what the story was about' (p. 11).

Possibly not, although his class and sense of his own background are major contributing factors to John's constant feelings of alienation and exclusion. Sharing rooms with Christopher Warner, a rugby-playing hearty from a minor public school, John desperately wants admission to Christopher's social world. He turns Christopher's schooldays into a romantic fantasy:

. . . it seemed to him that in their schooldays they had won more than he would ever win during the whole of his life. . . . As the picture grew in his mind, he ornamented it with little marginal additions, until in the end the thing was as unreal as a highly-coloured picture of an ancient battle . . . (pp. 57–8)

This utterly misguided impression of the school lives of Christopher and his friends in turn fosters John's fantasies of becoming a central figure in their world (pp. 61–2). Moreover his university contemporary who might be considered John's social equal, Whitbread, comes across as smug and grotesque, so that it is at least understandable that John does not feel friendly towards him.

Timms maintains that *Jill* is primarily about 'our tendency to make fantasies, and the dangers into which it leads us'.[6] But while the concept of class in the novel is largely confined to John's sense of exclusion from Christopher's world, which does point more in the direction of psychological need than of social comment or sociological analysis, we cannot help suspecting that the workings of John's imagination reach back into his education and are to some extent explained by it. The only person through whose eyes we see John (as opposed to John's visions of how others see him) is his schoolmaster, Mr Crouch. While Crouch is preparing John for the university scholarship examination it becomes clear that he is trying to create an ideal student to complement his own ideal conception of himself (pp. 65–85). Crouch's nature is succinctly explained by his university notes (p. 66), the tidy efficiency of which at once covers Crouch's essential emptiness and suppresses the sensual streak in his nature that longs for idleness and freedom. The psychological effects on both teacher and pupil of Crouch's attempt to teach John to assimilate literature in this way are revealing. From Crouch's point of view, 'It was like manipulating a powerful but delicate machine' (p. 77); he 'felt strongly as if a mechanical man he had painfully constructed had suddenly come to life' (p. 83). But Crouch feels cheated precisely because the 'life' is no more than the regular working of a conditioned mechanism:

Although Kemp worked hard and intelligently . . . he was a burden to teach. His character was almost purely negative: if there had come one spontaneous idea from him during all the span of their acquaintanceship, Mr. Crouch would have felt repaid, but the hesitancy and heaviness that he had imagined would wear off as the boy's imagination widened and deepened persisted month after month, until Mr. Crouch was forced to admit it was native to him and would never go. (p. 79)

[6] David Timms, *Philip Larkin*, Oliver and Boyd, Edinburgh 1973, p. 37.

John has become the monster to Crouch's Frankenstein, and Crouch cannot see that his own method of teaching has denied John the imaginative response that would so gratify himself. Rather than an indictment of the educational system, however, we are given a comment on Crouch as a particular type of person who is gradually losing any sense of purpose in his own life—a view that is corroborated later when we see him visiting John at Oxford (pp. 225–9). Nevertheless the fact that John's imaginative life suffers because of his education cannot be ignored; and that it is not followed up as much as it might be suggests that there is in *Jill*, in addition to everything else, a sociological novel that never got written.

John's starved imagination compensates by vividly pictorial fantasies. As his imaginary recreation of Christopher's world (quoted above) suggests, he constantly visualizes his imaginative responses. When he is having tea with Christopher and Mrs Warner, his desire to be Mrs Warner's son translates itself into a brilliant 'image' of her (p. 94); and when, having been depressed by the sight of himself in a shop-window he decides that he needs a bow-tie to smarten himself up, he has 'a sudden vision of the bow-tie, lying in a pool of light at the bottom of a lift-shaft, very tiny and distinct' (p. 98). Overhearing Christopher and his girl-friend Elizabeth say insulting and patronizing things about him, he 'sees' himself differently as a result of what they have 'shown' him; things come into 'focus', his vision of Christopher and his friends is 'refracted', and 'the words he had overheard shone in his mind in lacerating detail' (pp. 111–15).

The visual aspect of John's imagination is more central to the novel than these examples of local detail indicate. It can be used to place the central character, to establish him in relation to the broader scheme of the novel's values. He may be the hero (the word is Larkin's), although he is not the book's sole concern; and while the narrative voice does focus on his imaginative life it also moves outside it, and incorporates it within the scope of a broader view than that of John Kemp. By taking us outside John, and by allowing us to see him in a visualized setting, Larkin can give the reader an additional perspective. Thus, for example, at the very beginning of the novel:

John Kemp sat in the corner of an empty compartment in a train travelling over the last stretch of line before Oxford. It was nearly four o'clock on a Thursday in the middle of October, and the air had begun to thicken as it always does before a dusk in autumn. The sky had become stiff with opaque clouds. When they were clear of the gasometers, the wagons and blackened bridges of Banbury, he looked out over the fields, noticing the clumps of trees that sped by, whose dying leaves each had an individual colour, from palest ochre to nearly purple, so that each tree stood out distinctly as in spring. The hedges were still green, but the leaves of the convolvuli threaded through them had turned sickly yellow, and from a distance looked like late flowers. Little arms of rivers twisted through the meadows, lined with willows that littered the surface with leaves. The waters were spanned by empty footbridges. (p. 21)

From John we move out into the landscape, and (in the following paragraph) back into the railway carriage to focus once again on John: 'He was an undersized boy, eighteen years old, with a pale face and soft pale hair brushed childishly from left to right'. We are both seeing John and seeing with him. We are given the landscape as John would see it and we are told of the things he notices, but we are being introduced to John at the same time. Our first sight of John, in the context of this landscape, is conditioned by a tone of emotional bleakness that is central to the context of John's whole existence. For we see a landscape of death, and although John sees it as well, he is placed in it and is thus part of it. The descriptive movement from the 'empty compartment' to the 'empty footbridges' incorporates thickening air, stiffening sky, blackened bridges, dying or sickly yellow leaves; and as the last adjective of the passage repeats the first one the major impression communicated to the reader is a feeling of emptiness which is experienced by John at the same time as it surrounds him. From the opening page it is obvious to the reader that John has little chance, and the entire book is coloured by this deterministic attitude.

The next day we see John pondering university life:

What was the rest of the University doing? Looking round, he saw dozens of students, pushing into teashops or bookshops, wearing new college scarves and talking at the top of their voices, and to get away from them he walked down the High Street as far as the river and stood on the broad bridge. From there he could see trees on the river banks and the water running quickly under stone walls. Farther up, a swan plunged its neck deep into the weeds, and, lingering by the balustrade of the bridge, he lost himself for a moment in the tranquillity of the scene, watching the dead leaves drifting away with the current. (p. 46)

'He saw . . . he could see . . . he lost himself': the progression of verbs recreates John's bewilderment, which is simultaneously visualized by the reader. Once again, we are shown both John, and what he sees. By setting the apparent purpose and bustling vitality of the students against the drifting dead leaves, and by associating John with the latter (the participles at the end of the passage blend him unobtrusively into the scene he is watching), Larkin again associates John with loneliness and lack of purpose which we are invited to share. The sharpness of descriptive focus serves to manipulate the reader as well as the hero.

Such examples could be multiplied, ranging as they do from straightforward analogy between setting and mood (p. 97) to moments of realization or decision (pp. 170, 193–4). The very precision of these passages works to emphasize John's sense of alienation, and nowhere is this more effectively done than in the account of his visit home to Huddlesford following reports of an air-raid on the town. Looking through the window of his parents' home, John realizes the extent to which he is now shut out from his former life (p. 215); and his feeling of being excluded informs all aspects of this novel, which abounds in images of doors, barriers, and windows. In this passage any class emphasis is played down. John's home, like the railway compartment in which we first met him, is empty, and significantly so because his most pressing need is for human warmth and contact with other people. It is this from which he feels excluded; and it is this feeling that he is impotent to involve himself in the lives of others that inspires his fantasy of Jill.

John's failure to weave himself into the lives of Christopher and his circle and his failure to get them to like and accept him result in his total withdrawal into himself, and in the creation of a fantasy that comes to dominate his whole existence. Christopher (somewhat implausibly) takes an interest in the fact that John has a sister. To increase this interest John writes himself a letter from his sister Jill, and leaves it lying around in the hope that Christopher will see and read it. (John's real sister, whose name we are not told, actually teaches in Manchester. The imaginary Jill, however, is being educated at 'Willow Gables School', and thus belongs in Christopher's social world rather than in John's.) But Christopher is less interested than John likes to imagine, and simply forgets the whole business. For John, however, the idea gains a momentum of its own and changes his entire perspective: 'Everything indeed seemed altered, as if he had ignorantly twisted his tongue round a magic formula and was watching the world change before his eyes' (p. 119). He writes letters to Jill about events that have actually taken place, yet always brings himself to the fore in roles of domination and control. He even writes a story about her. And when none of this satisfies him any longer, he projects himself into her and takes on her identity by writing her diary.

His pictorial imagination enables John to visualize her: 'her image grew clearer in his mind: she was fifteen, and slight, her long fine dark honey-coloured hair fell to her shoulders and was bound with a white ribbon' (p. 135).[7] However hard he tries to imagine her, he never gets beyond self-dramatization; and one day it becomes clear to him that Jill is less a person than the embodiment of a feeling about innocence:

> The sensation he had was of looking intently into the centre of a pure white light: he seemed to see the essence of Jill . . . He thought he saw exactly what she was and how he should express it: the word was *innocent*, one he had used dozens of times in his own mind and yet until that moment never understood. (p. 152)[8]

John's conception of innocence is explained only by implication. It apparently means at once 'untainted' and 'unattainable', set apart from the reality of everyday experience. And having suddenly lighted on the idea, he finds its human form in a bookshop.

The sight of a girl who incarnates his ideal so perfectly gives him 'a shock that could not have been greater if a brick had been thrown through the plate-glass shop-window' (p. 156). This girl now becomes an obsession for John. There is always something dream-like about her, for she seems always to be 'drifting away' from him, and events have 'the deliberate tantalizing quality of a dream' or 'the deliberation of a mirage' (pp. 157, 158, 166). Unattainable as she is, John's feelings for her are emphatically not sexual. Utterly horrified by the sight of Christopher shaving himself in preparation for his anticipated seduction of Elizabeth, John is aghast to think that his own quest for Jill might end in any such way. In his fantasy life things like that do not happen, and consequently Jill becomes for him the gateway to a world where such squalid things need never take place: 'Never must she be allowed to go outside her own life. And then through her he might enter this life, this other innocent life she led' (p. 170). This notion of innocence and an innocent life cannot possibly be realized, notwithstanding its clarity for John. Jill cannot come into his life, but by entering hers he can shelter from all the things that threaten and frighten him. He has simply retreated further into himself.

The complete unreality of John's thoughts underlines the dangerous potency of his starved and stunted imagination, and of course the impossibility of such dreams ever coming to fulfilment is an essential aspect of their attraction for him. Not until after the climax of the book, when John drunkenly kisses Jill, does the novel offer any direct comment

[7] See also p. 121.
[8] See also p. 135: 'She was a hallucination of innocence'.

on the related strands of illusion, imagination, and fulfilment; but when the comment comes it is deterministic, and it is rendered visually for both John and the reader. He has had a dream starkly dramatizing 'the boredom of no longer loving':

> And this dream showed that love died, whether fulfilled or unfulfilled. He grew confused whether she had accepted him or not, since the result was the same: and as this confusion increased, it spread to fulfilment or unfulfilment, which merged and became inseparable. The difference between them vanished.
>   He was watching the trees, the tops of which he could just see through the window . . . Endlessly, this way and that, they were buffeted and still bore up again to their full height. They seemed tireless. Sometimes they were bent so low that they passed out of sight, leaving the square of white sky free for a second, but then they would be back again, clashing their proud branches together like the antlers of furious stags. (p. 242)

The questions that the novel asks us to ponder here are concerned with the relationship between the life of the imagination and the life of factual reality, and at this point the narrative voice has taken over completely; for although John is 'watching' too, the images are coming straight at the reader: John is barely even a medium between narrator and reader. The effect is of the narrator directly addressing his reader, with an occasional nod in the direction of his central character: 'Let him take this course, or this course, but still behind the mind, on some other level, the way he had rejected was being simultaneously worked out and the same conclusion was being reached' (p. 243). So transparent is John at this point that the philosophy of determinism we are being offered is given only the most flimsy of disguises as the central character's realization of the nature of his own experience: 'Was he not freed, for the rest of his life, from choice? . . . What control could he hope to have over the maddened surface of things?' (p. 243). John is supposedly asking the questions of himself, but on another level the narrator is asking them of the reader. What the imagination suggests as fulfilment is as true as it may be impossible, and there is no difference between fulfilment and its opposite because the brutal fact is that love dies. And yet the novel raises more questions than it answers, if only because the image of the relentlessly tossing trees suggests not only determinism but also a degree of heroic self-assertion in the face of that determinism. Larkin has said of his time at Oxford, the Oxford of wartime austerity: 'At an age when self-importance would have been normal, events cut us ruthlessly down to size' (p. 12). Events throughout *Jill* certainly cut John Kemp down to size—almost every episode ends in his humiliation—yet Larkin is obviously fascinated by the response of the human imagination to that.

Like *Jill*, *A Girl in Winter* is also primarily concerned with the imaginative life of its central character. If John feels somewhat out of place in Oxford, Katherine Lind has more reason not to feel at home in her job in a provincial English library. Neither permanent, nor a junior, nor a senior, and not even English, 'she was foreign and had no proper status there' (p. 25). *A Girl in Winter* is also constructed more tightly than its predecessor. It covers a single day in Katherine's life, but its tripartite structure enables the novel to glance back into her past. Thus the second section is cast as a flashback to her previous visit to England as a schoolgirl, when she stayed one summer with the family of her penfriend, Robin Fennel. And in the third section Larkin closely reviews the major stages in Katherine's emotional development as he brings us back to the present.

Katherine's memory of her earlier visit is the most potent force in her life. Her imagination, like that of John, has created certain illusions, although in her case these are concerned with a memory of the past rather than a fantasy of the future. The reason the episode is so attractive to her is made quite clear: 'It was the only period of her life that had not been spoiled by later events, and she found that she could draw upon it hearteningly, remembering when she had been happy, and ready to give and take, instead of unwilling to give, and finding nothing worth taking'. And she wants to see the Fennels again because 'It was as if she hoped they would warm back to life a part of her that had been frozen' (p. 185). The harsh falsity of this wish, which amounts to a desire to retreat into the past, is reinforced by the contrast between that idyllic summer and the present bitter winter's day. The past remains preserved in her memory as a static imprint, like the photograph taken by Mr Fennel: 'And so the image of them standing and sitting in relaxed attitudes in the evening sun was pressed onto the negative for all eternity' (p. 162).

The twists and turns of the narrative reverse the expectations of Katherine's imagination. As a schoolgirl she had built up a picture of her penfriend Robin Fennel that failed utterly to conform to the reality, and this disturbed her (p. 77). Nor was the English countryside at all what she expected (p. 80). The physical desire she later felt for Robin shattered her adolescent idea of love as protective and enclosing (p. 127). In the present, her meeting with Robin fails completely to answer her expectations (pp. 226–35). And by a chance discovery on this winter's day she has learned that the loathing she feels for Mr Anstey, her superior in the library, is quite unjustified. Knowledge of his personal life has forced her to modify her opinion of him: 'For her conception of him as a hostile cartoon she had to substitute a person who had and could evoke feelings, who would undertake the support of an old woman, and on whose account she had seen another crying' (pp. 204–5). This constant pattern of disappointment or of expectations not being fulfilled reminds us of John Kemp, but in this novel the *motif* is at once more concentrated and more pointed. Katherine is both older and tougher than John, and in her case the continuous process of having her imaginative conceptions overturned results in a steady growth of maturity. At the end of the novel, after we have reviewed her entire emotional development, we are made to feel that she has attained a mature and realistic outlook on life, or at least a mature acceptance of its processes. Thus the ending of *A Girl in Winter* is less equivocal than that of *Jill*.

The moral centre of the novel is to be found in the second and fifth chapters of the final section, where Larkin describes the workings of Katherine's mind as she tries to come to terms with the condition of loneliness that she finds everywhere about her. The most reflective parts of a day which she has come to think of as 'an odyssey in a dream' (p. 179), these chapters chart an odyssey of self-discovery: they reach back into her past, and lead up to her reunion with Robin. We are shown the various alternating stages of hope and reduced expectation experienced by Katherine since she arrived in England for the second time, and as these are incorporated into the present we see Katherine's progression to a degree of realization and knowledge. A fine balance of distance and involvement in the narrative voice enables Larkin simultaneously to show us Katherine and to tell us about her in a more sustained and less fragmentary manner than that in which John Kemp was presented. What we are told about the workings of her consciousness is illustrated in detail by a range of figurative reference. On her return to England, Katherine's life was at first a nightmare of unfamiliarity:

> It was as if the world had been turned round, like innumerable bits of reversible stage scenery. Quite frequently she felt moments of stark terror at the strangeness of things, at the way all had collapsed, presumably as a cat will go mad upon the ruins of its suddenly-destroyed home. There was only one sure thing. She was still alive. The rest was like walking across a plaster ceiling. (p. 181)

The similes expand and illustrate the related ideas of loneliness and dislocation by gradually reducing the stature of Katherine. First, her situation is implicitly compared with that of an actress, whose actions are predetermined but which guarantee a certain degree of familiarity, which is however destroyed by an unexpected movement of the stage scenery. Then the shattering of familiarity is conveyed by comparing her terror with that of an uncomprehending animal driven mad by the destruction of familiar things. And finally, she is reduced to the smallness of an inverted insect walking upside down across a ceiling.

It is impossible to know whether these similes refer to Katherine's thoughts about herself, or whether they are the narrator's means of explaining her feelings to the reader. With reference to the first sentence of the passage quoted, for example, it is quite likely that the world might have seemed 'turned round' to Katherine's dislocated imagination; but the 'unexpected movement of stage scenery' is probably a further explanation added by the narrator. In any case, the narrator's sympathetic involvement in her predicament enables him to explain her feelings figuratively, and to make them accessible to the reader: the essential thing is his struggle to illustrate graphically and tangibly the state of mind of his central character.

By way of coping with this progressive erosion of her sense of self Katherine reduces everything to its simplest terms. The consequence of her attempt to suppress every reference to her former life is that she creates an unreal present, yet her eventual acknowledgement of this unreality shocks her into a recognition 'that even if her old life had been waiting for her, she no longer wanted to return to it' (p. 182). At this point Katherine comes to believe in the maturity of her own perspectives:

> For she knew, now, that in most lives there had to come a break, when the past dropped away and the maturity it had enclosed for so long stood painfully upright. It came through death or disaster, or even through a love-affair that with the best will in the world on both sides went wrong. . . . But once the break was made, as though continually-trickling sand had caused a building to slip suddenly on its foundations so that perhaps one single ornament fell to the floor, life ceased to be a confused stumbling from one illumination to another, a series of unconnected clearings in a tropical forest, and became a flat landscape, wry and rather small, with a few unforgettable landmarks somewhat resembling a stretch of fen-land, where an occasional dyke or broken fence shows up for miles, and the sails of a mill turn all day long in the steady wind. (p. 183)

The first sentences of this paragraph refer directly to Katherine's thoughts, but the last one, which contains no mention of her, develops into a series of similes whose purpose is to illuminate each other. As the passage develops it leaves Katherine behind. The figurative language takes on a life of its own, with no *specific* reference to her experience, and it comes as a slight jolt when the next paragraph begins 'She knew', and we have to cast our minds back.

The descriptive explanation of her thoughts has, in effect, abandoned her. It may be, of course, that the naturalistic settings in which Larkin placed John Kemp have in this novel been internalized, but it remains uncertain whether they are part of the substance of Katherine's thoughts or the narrator's way of telling us about those thoughts. In any case the fact that the narrator may occasionally interpose himself and mask our view of Katherine Lind is not a negative criticism of the novel, for the protagonist is being used by the narrator to order his perceptions about human emotions. As in *Jill*, it is all vividly pictorial, and to show us the way in which Katherine thinks about life is also to let us look into her mind: 'For the world seemed to have moved off a little, and to have lost its immediacy, as a bright pattern will fade in many washings. It was like a painting of a winter landscape in neutral colours, or a nocturne in many greys of the riverside, yet not so beautiful as either. Like a person who is beginning to go physically colour-blind she was disturbed' (p. 184). This last simile is surely for the reader only: Katherine obviously does not think she is going colour-blind, and it is unlikely that she would draw an analogy between her feelings and the physical condition of colour-blindness. Katherine's perceptions are rendered to the reader by the narrator in terms of figurative visual perceptions that take us beyond her own particular situation.

The landscape she sees may be dull, but it is all of a piece. Reduced expectations of what life may offer leave little scope for disappointment, and her viewpoint is apparently endorsed even though it does involve a conception of human life as largely determined by things outside human wishes. Indeed, the notion of determinism here is crucial: 'And she had believed for a long time that a person's life is directed mainly by their actions, and these in turn are directed by their personality, which is not self-chosen in the first place and modifies itself quite independently of their wishes afterwards' (p. 185). The idea makes a mockery of intention and desire, and casts a shadow of pathos over human feelings: 'Her feelings were like a flight of birds that swoop over to one corner of a field and then stop, all trembling equidistantly in the air, and then come streaming back, like a banner tossed first one way, then the other' (p. 178). So naturally does one simile flow from another that one is scarcely shocked to find human feelings compared to an inanimate object at the mercy of the wind.[9]

The tragic paradox is that as external events and circumstances over which one has no control work against the potency of human wishes, so the wish-fulfilling drives in the human imagination exert themselves more strongly. Katherine's discoveries are more valuable than those of John Kemp because they are more discriminating, and also because her recognition of her own loneliness and isolation has to be seen as an acceptance of what the novel offers as an essential truth about the human condition:

> She thought of the darkness covering not only these miles of streets around her, but also of the shores, the beaches, and the acres of tossing sea that she had crossed, which divided her from her proper home. At least her birthplace and the street she walked in were sharing the same night, however many unfruitful miles were between them. And there too people would keep indoors, and not think of much beyond the fires that warmed them, for the same winter lay stiffly across the whole continent. (p. 224)

Larkin does place her in a setting at the same time as he keeps us aware of what she sees and thinks about, but the whole thrust of the passage is beyond the personal. Winter is more than just seasonal coldness; coupled with the wartime black-out it becomes a condition of isolation affecting the whole of humanity. Like the snow at the end of Joyce's 'The Dead', it encompasses all. Yet precisely because darkness, silence, and enclosure are communal, they minimize Katherine's *personal* alienation and are even vaguely comforting. She may be divided from her 'proper home', but she is reminded of it; and this passage also recalls the opening chapter of the novel (pp. 11–12) which, ostensibly describing a winter's morning, actually hints at the human need to endure: 'Life had to be carried on, in no matter what circumscribed way' (p. 11). This opening chapter, in marked contrast to the opening of *Jill*, does not even hint at the central character. The cold, both at the opening of *A Girl in Winter* and in the passage just quoted, is seen to affect all levels of life, but it has to be accepted and grappled with, and human endeavour must continue in the face of it.

The central character is less relevant to this novel than to *Jill*. Larkin is capable of presenting character superbly and dramatically—Mr Anstey

[9] Timms thinks some of these similes are redundant (Timms, p. 51); but the apparent redundancy is at least partly explained by the narrator's movement away from the character.

is a case in point—but this is not his major concern. The scope of the novel's figurative frame of reference embraces Larkin's central interest in the quality of Katherine's imaginative life which, held up as a model of human mental processes generally, is intended to draw attention to fundamental aspects of human living. These concern the relationship between the human imagination and such things as curb and limit it. This is surely not a negative focus—for a recognition of such limitations is essential to human living—any more than the novel's conclusion, as Katherine and Robin sleep together, is pessimistic:

> There was the snow, and her watch ticking. So many snowflakes, so many seconds. As time passed they seemed to mingle in their minds, heaping up into a vast shape that might be a burial mound, or the cliff of an iceberg whose summit is out of sight. Into its shadow dreams crowded, full of conceptions and stirrings of cold, as if icefloes were moving down a lightless channel of water. They were going in orderly slow procession, moving from darkness further into darkness, allowing no suggestion that their order should be broken, or that one day, however many years distant, the darkness would begin to give place to light.
>
> Yet their passage was not saddening. Unsatisfied dreams rose and fell about them, crying out against their implacability, but in the end glad that such order, such destiny, existed. Against this knowledge, the heart, the will, and all that made for protest, could at last sleep. (p. 248)

We are given no firm clues about what will happen to Robin and Katherine, and therefore the end of the narrative is clouded in uncertainty. Nevertheless the ending serves to remind us of the muted expectations life offers, and from that point of view the uncertainty is important and relevant. Like the novel as a whole, this closing passage moves beyond the characters without allowing us to forget them. It is, for example, frequently difficult to find a precise referent for the pronoun *they* and its forms; for although we may be tempted automatically to assume its reference to the lovers this may be grammatically impossible, or at best qualified by possible ambiguity. Personalities disappear or are gathered up by the generalizing nouns, and the human is placed in a context of balanced determinism, which is the note on which the novel ends. Dreams and unsatisfied longings are inevitable and even necessary, yet we survive in spite of them and the protest they raise; and the fact of death itself constitutes a kind of order. Neither novel presents us with conclusive solutions, on either the narrative or the philosophical level, but it should be stressed that in neither novel is a deterministic view of life presented in such a way as to appear wholly negative or pessimistic. Whatever the limitations of human choice and the delusive nature of hope life still leaves scope for human effort, and however elusive happiness might be its possibility is not denied.

Larkin has described both his novels as 'oversized poems . . . written with intense care for detail'.[10] This care for detail has ensured that the language of both books is more precise as well as more evocative than the shadowy diction of *The North Ship*. *Jill* abounds in greater incident than *A Girl in Winter*, and greater attention is paid to more characters than in the later novel, but the power of *A Girl in Winter* comes from its increased conciseness. John Bayley's generous praise of this novel as 'one of the finest and best sustained prose poems in the language'[11] is well merited. Generally, it can be said, the novels remedied the lack of direction that was such a disturbing feature of the early poetry, and in both of them we can see the narrative voice organizing Larkin's own perceptions around those of the central character. The ordered pictorialism of many of the metaphorically suggestive descriptive passages—and the opening chapter of *A Girl in Winter* itself has the quality of 'a formal painting' which belongs to the landscape it describes—shows us the narrator moving beyond the central character to a more direct enunciation of his own perceptions, and in the proliferation of such passages we can see Larkin outgrowing the need for another mediating, fictional consciousness. Explaining his reasons for giving up novel writing, Larkin told Ian Hamilton: 'I suppose I must have lost interest in other people, or perhaps I was only pretending to be interested in them'.[12] It is certainly true that Larkin's interest in John Kemp and Katherine Lind was an unconscious means to self-definition. The authorial consciousness developed to a point where such characters were no longer needed, and the author no longer needed to write novels. In future the brief assumption of a mask was to replace the extended treatment of a single character, and such masks as were required could be incorporated within poetic forms.

Technically, therefore, the novels were extremely valuable to Larkin. They also introduce the concerns and interests that pervade the subsequent poetry: the difficulty of ever fully knowing or coming to terms with what we think of as 'the self'; the transient nature of human emotion; our constant awareness of death; and the limitless capacity of

[10] Ian Hamilton interview, see n. 2 above, p. 248.
[11] John Bayley, 'Too Good for This World', *TLS*, 21 June 1974, p. 654.
[12] Ian Hamilton interview, p. 248.

mankind for illusion and self-deception. All these had their beginnings in *Jill* and *A Girl in Winter*, both of which are extended examinations of the deceptions their central characters create for themselves. Although these themes took root in the novels, their offshoots required further and more varied modes of cultivation and development. And the first substantial harvest of Larkin's return to poetry was *The Less Deceived*.

II

The Less Deceived

The diversity of the twenty-nine poems in this book is underpinned by the notion of deceptions, the varieties of deception we visit upon ourselves rather than the ways in which we may be deceived by others. The human capacity for self-deception is exposed as almost limitless. It is shown to be a consequence of our tendency to project our desires onto our lives, and then allow our lives to be governed by them. The book's title comes from the poem 'Deceptions' (p. 37), which encapsulates many of Larkin's concerns:

> For you would hardly care
> That you were less deceived, out on that bed,
> Than he was, stumbling up the breathless stair
> To burst into fulfilment's desolate attic.

This poem is a commentary on its headnote which reproduces a girl's account of her 'ruin', from Mayhew's *London Labour and the London Poor*. At first glance the poem is offering something patently absurd for our contemplation: the girl, drugged and raped though she was, was actually less deceived than the man who raped her. Bad as it was for her, the poem suggests, it was worse for the rapist in that he had more illusions about the experience. She was deceived by him, whereas his deception was self-imposed; and because he deceived himself, hers was the lesser of the two deceptions.

If this seems a clinically detached attitude to rape, it should be observed that Larkin's portrayal of the girl is wonderfully sympathetic. Without in any sense offering her consolation he precisely and exactly evokes her feelings by taking us inside her mind as she awakens to her discovery. Linked by the metaphorically realized ideas of violence, pain, and brutality, and leaving us in no doubt as to the horror of the experience, the opening and closing sentences of the first stanza distance the girl's emotions in the past; but as the central second sentence recreates the girl's grief, so the present tense both brings to life the girl's experience and dramatizes the truth of the poet's statement in the first line, 'I can taste the grief'. And of course his sympathetic identification is established not only by what he says, but also in the metaphorical relationship between his own 'taste' and the grief 'gulped' by the girl. The subsequent sense-impressions recall the world to which she must return and thus intensify her consciousness of shame, an intensification heightened by the hurrying movement over the line-ending of the 'brisk brief/Worry of wheels'. The submerged pun on 'bridal' economically keeps the impression of sound in the reader's (and the girl's) mind as it allows us to glimpse her realization of the consequences: for who will want to marry her now?

In the second stanza the poem gets more discursive, moving away from the reality of pain to images of psychological expectation. But the precision of the first stanza remains in the mind, and lends concreteness to the more abstract statements of the second part of the poem. If the poet, in opposing 'desire' and 'suffering', is really to convince us that 'suffering is exact', then this exactness has to be established; and this is precisely what the first stanza has done by merging the narrative consciousness with that of the girl. Desire, on the other hand, is no more than an unrealized idea. The exactness of suffering is a measure of its reality, whereas the rapist's idea of fulfilment only leads him breathlessly to emptiness and desolation.

There are traces of the novelistic manner here. The story or incident is only significant in so far as it provides a springboard for analysis of consciousness or emotion. The confident and central presence of the poet enables him to blend his own consciousness with that of his subject, and then to detach himself for authoritative comment. He leads us firmly from the girl's mind to a statement about the deceptive capacities of the imagination, a statement firmly supported by the imaginative rendition of the girl's grief. The unity and development of the poem are unobtrusively structured by its rhymes, which also underscore the meaning. In the first stanza the rhymes draw together the different time-perspectives of the poem by linking the first and third sentences of the poem to the second one, thereby also establishing an enfolding consciousness from which authoritative statements can emerge. And in the second stanza the first rhyme sound ('dare'/'where') persists throughout, ensuring stability through the developing syntactical pattern of statement, question, and explanation.

By making us aware of the self-deluding tendencies of the human mind, this poem draws the underlying significance from an incident in nineteenth-century social history. The commentary extends the significance of the incident far beyond its historical context. This manner is typical of much of Larkin's work: his poems frequently consist of a single event or image around which a commentary has been constructed, the purpose of which is to make explicit the meaning of the central symbolic image or event. The reader is therefore being simultaneously shown and told in a way that is reminiscent of the presentation of John Kemp and Katherine Lind. Rarely, in subsequent volumes, has Larkin used figurative language so overtly, for many poems in *The Less Deceived* achieve their effect by means of a highly self-conscious use of image and symbol.

'Triple Time' (p. 35) is a more abstract poem than 'Deceptions', but its manner is similar. Instead of a narrative, however, we are given a series of related visual metaphors for time. And whereas in 'Deceptions' the poet is directly addressing the girl he has read about in Mayhew, here he is addressing no one in particular (although the 'we' of the final stanza draws the reader into the poem). Time is shown to us from three perspectives: present, past, and future. There are also three stanzas and three sentences, but after the opening stanza-sentence, sentence and stanza no longer coincide. The second sentence, which cuts across the second and third stanzas in such a way as to incorporate statements about both the future and the past, therefore suggests their similar effect on the human consciousness, and also allows Larkin to use the stanza-break dramatically to remind us that the gap between future and past is largely illusory. As so often happens in Larkin's poetry, too, the final sentence moves to a detached statement whose brutal finality sums up the poem: 'On this we blame our last/Threadbare perspectives, seasonal decrease'. The recurrent 'this' rivets the poem's focus on the present as the place from which we cannot escape, but following its particularized reference in the opening lines of the poem it gradually lapses into vagueness as that to which it refers becomes hazy. As the first stanza makes clear, the present is itself informed by unreality: 'Like a reflection' implies reality at one remove. The word 'reflection' is crucial to the poem; it refers not only to a process of consciousness, but also to the relationship of future and past. The meaning of the first stanza is enacted by a mimetic play on the visual meaning of this word:

> This empty street, this sky to blandness scoured,
> This air, a little indistinctive with autumn
> Like a reflection, constitute the present—
> A time traditionally soured,
> A time unrecommended by event.

The first two lines mirror each other syntactically, just as the syntax of the fifth line reflects the syntax of the fourth. Furthermore the syntactical relationships within the first and second and fourth and fifth lines set these pairs of lines in relationship to each other. The reflection is not exact, but the relationship serves to set out visually the poem's point about imprisonment within the present; for the central line of the stanza, the object of the sentence, and the central idea of isolation, appropriately stand alone.

The second line of each stanza is also isolated by having no rhyming partner. Such technical adroitness in manipulating the poem's form to mirror its sense is brought to life by the language of the senses—touching and tasting, seeing and hearing—and the modification of the visual imagery to a somewhat incongruous glimpse of the past as a sheep feeding reminds us that we may indeed hunger for the past. Also, by taking up the pun on the unusual word '*lamb*ent' in the previous stanza, this image dramatically forces us to look back as we are in the very act of reading the poem. And Larkin does not leave it at that: 'cropped' and 'fleece' weave the metaphor further into the linguistic texture of the poem, until the idea is at last worn out by the final 'threadbare perspectives'.

Against the barrenness of the present is set the elusive promise of the future, and the unfulfilled promise of the past. The 'neglected chances' may seem real only in retrospect, because 'forebore' suggests that neglect at the time was deliberate choice rather than chance omission. As for John Kemp and Katherine Lind, the idea of plenitude takes shape in the human mind as images of what we lack. Perspective does not bring significance.[1] Rather, it makes us aware of intentions gone astray, and the human imagination is both fantasizing and reductive.

This poem simultaneously crystallizes and comments upon some of the most threadbare habits of the human consciousness. The bad habit of expectancy is also the subject of 'Next, Please' (p. 20), which likewise uses a central metaphor to carry the weight of its assertions. Once again the deception involved is self-deception, and refers to our expectation 'that age will perform the promises of youth, and that the deficiencies of the present day will be supplied by the morrow'.[2] The poem forces us to recognize that most things are attractive only in anticipation, which is why we are tempted to expect the future to compensate for the deficiencies and disappointments of the past. Finally, the apparently endless 'sparkling armada of promises' turns eerily into a ship of death,

[1] See 'Whatever Happened?', p. 25.
[2] *Rasselas*, ch. i.

'towing at her back/A huge and birdless silence'. With the compulsion of a dream-image, this transformation shocks us into recognition of the hollowness of most of our waking dreams. The pun on 'bluff', too, exposes the pretence, but the poem's substance is dramatized most effectively by its rhyme and rhythm. The contributory effect of a simple verse-form is quite remarkable. At the opening, for example: 'Always too eager for the future, we/Pick up bad habits of expectancy'. We are immediately enmeshed in a pattern of expectancy. The grammatical subject of this first sentence, 'we', hurries us over the line-ending in community of interests with the poet, until we find our rhyming complement at the end of the sentence and at the end of the second line, in 'expectancy'. The poem is stylistically encouraging us to adopt the habit it actually warns us against, but the satisfying completeness of this opening couplet is exceptional: the poem's ulterior purpose is to undeceive. There are many breaks of syntax or punctuation just before a line-ending, so that immediately after the conclusion of a grammatical unit or a syntactical movement a fresh pattern of expectancy is set up which refuses to allow the couplet to rest in its own completion:

> . . . and the figurehead with golden tits
> Arching our way, it never anchors; it's
> No sooner present than it turns to past.

The technical enactment here is superb: the contraction 'it's' chimes with its antecedent and then, bustling us on to the third line, stings us into a dramatic realization of how quickly the present does become the past. The rhyming-pattern generates a sense of expectation which, when fulfilled, is both fleeting and hollow; for at the very moment we are experiencing it, the syntax is propelling us on to the next line and setting up new expectations. In addition the shortened fourth line of each stanza helps to slow down the progression of the poem, as well as frequently to begin a fresh syntactical movement (as in the line following those quoted above, which begins a new sentence). The cross-changes of pace and movement generated by rhythm and syntax deny the logic of expectation, and finally usher in the death ship.

However, the poem's dramatic enactment of its idea is focused on the visual quality of its central image. 'No Road' (p. 26) also functions largely in terms of its given image. Here, the metaphor of a disused road is used to convey thoughts about a relationship that has apparently outlived its purpose. There is no pretence that the metaphor is naturalistic, any more than there is in 'Next, Please' or 'Triple Time'. We are simply asked to visualize something in terms of something else, the poet assumes the reader's immediate mental adjustment to the poem's metaphorical level, and commentary is integrated with description. When the commentary disappears we are left with psychological allegory. The subject of 'Wires' (p. 27) is human limitations, but the poem says nothing about these directly. Instead it works fully and solely through the symbolic implications of its title. The two quatrains do not rhyme internally, but as Timms has pointed out 'the rhyme scheme of the second stanza is a mirror image of that of the first, so that the last line of the poem rhymes with the first, the next last with the second, and so on'.[3] Moreover, as our eyes follow the syntax of the second sentence across the stanza break, in going 'Beyond the wires' our experience of reading leads us to 'blunder up against the wires' into a non-rhyme on the same word. With reference to the entire poem, the rhyming field establishes an enclosure. Reversal is also an organizing principle of the poem, not only in the rhyme or in the polarization of young against old, but also in the word-order. In the last line of the poem the relative positions of the adjectives we encountered in the first line have been reversed; and while this has been happening the poem's thrust has gradually become internalized, 'prairies' and 'fences' having been turned into 'limits' and 'senses'. Most of us would rather be elsewhere—'anywhere'—than 'here'. Maturity is nothing less than recognition and awareness of limitations which the cramped form and manner of the poem impose on the reader's imagination.

We are never in any doubt, either in 'Wires' or in the poems previously discussed, about the application of the central images. The insistence on the metaphor here, and the integration of its meaning with other technical aspects of the poem, ensure that we do not need the interpreting voice that guided us through 'Deceptions' or 'Triple Time'. But not all the poems that dispense with commentary are as easy to fathom as 'Wires', for the very absence of commentary can render some poems elusive and cryptic. The imagery in 'Dry-Point' (p. 19) is once again almost wholly visual, but even the introduction of prosaic Birmingham fails to provide a satisfactory basis for a convincing and consistent interpretation. George Hartley, in what was the first published analysis of this poem, says: 'Directly addressed to a personification of sex, the poem's "occasion" is the disillusionment following the sexual act and its "theme" the impossibility of reaching any kind of fulfilment through sexual love'.

[3] David Timms, *Philip Larkin*, Oliver and Boyd, Edinburgh 1973, pp. 70–1.

Larkin has recently said in an interview that this poem has given him 'endless trouble' in the form of enquiries about its meaning, and his own brief explanation of the poem—'how awful sex is and how we want to get away from it'—does support George Hartley's reading.[4] Larkin's comment also illuminates much of the language of the poem, but the ambiguity of the title, whether intended or not, has made the poem hard for some to enter (dry-point is a method of etching).[5] It is therefore at least possible that the poem refers to some aspects of the creative as well as the sexual urge. The building-up and subsequent collapse of illusions, of whatever kind, in the first two stanzas suggests a connection with other poems in the book, although what the 'bare and sunscrubbed room' of the final stanza refers to is no more clear than if the 'you' of that stanza refers back to the 'time-honoured irritant' of the opening line. Whether the poem has to do with sex, or with creative power, it evokes a notion of imaginative process which never fulfils itself, yet its total meaning remains more oblique than is usually the case with Larkin's poetry. 'Absences' (p. 40) also works through a metaphor that has no obvious reference beyond itself. The subject—the poet's fascination with what familiar places are like when he is not there—is not made sufficiently accessible. The poem conveys an impression of endless flux in which nothing is fixed or certain, but this contributes to a lack of fixity which leaves the poem swimming in unsatisfactory fluidity. Like 'Dry-Point', 'Absences' centres on visual images which are not developed in close enough conjunction with the things to which they refer. The most potent absence is the absence of an authoritative centre.

So far we have ranged from poems such as 'Deceptions' and 'Triple Time', in which the poet establishes himself as an omniscient narrator without whose presence the poem would fall apart, through poems such as 'Next, Please' and 'No Road' which contain both a central metaphor and an explanatory interpretation of it, to poems such as 'Wires' and 'Dry-Point', in which there is no interpreting presence and where we have to work things out for ourselves. We have seen the poet, or projections of the poet, gradually disappear, which is the appropriate place to begin

[4] John Haffenden, 'The True and the Beautiful: a conversation with Philip Larkin', *The London Magazine*, 20, Nos 1–2 (April/May 1980), pp. 81–95 at p. 85. George Hartley's analysis of this poem, entitled 'No Right of Entry', is in the Larkin issue of *Phoenix*, 11/12, pp. 105–9.

[5] Margaret Blum, in a detailed application of methods of etching to the poem, argues that it 'uses an etching metaphor to create an allegory of the life-cycle of man'; *Explicator*, 32 (1974), Item 48. Rosenthal thinks this is one of Larkin's better poems: see *The New Poets*, pp. 239–40.

discussing the complex question of Larkin's fluctuating relationship with the various speakers of his poems.

Larkin has said: 'Generally my poems are related ... to my own personal life, but by no means always, since I can imagine horses I have never seen or the emotions of a bride without ever having been a woman or married'.[6] Such imaginative projection often requires a speaker or *persona* necessarily distinct from the poet. This comment makes specific reference to 'Wedding Wind' (p. 15), one of the poems printed in *Poets of the 1950s*, and the most obvious example in *The Less Deceived* of the use of a speaker who cannot be equated with the poet speaking in his own voice. This is Larkin's only poem with a recognizably female speaker, and its remarkable attempt at sexual empathy creates a tremendous feeling of exhilaration and uncomprehending wonder. Her words transcend the mundane details of the poem (although these details are very important), and the poem is all the more effective because she finds herself curiously detached from the process in which she is so intimately involved. The plenitude of sexual love is established by the 'elemental' features of the poem: by fire, by water, by the final image of worship which is at once ritualistic and wholly natural, and of course by the fullness and energy of the wind. In fact these things are precisely the means by which the poet stamps his own presence on the poem, for they provide the reader with enough hints to interpret the experiences and feelings of the poem in a way that the woman speaking is unable to do. She cannot intellectualize the process in which she is physically participating, but her unconscious awareness of its significance nevertheless emerges from the poem. Of course she is not stupid, and she is certainly presented with great sympathy, but she is also transparent; and thus we can perceive the elemental nature of her experience more clearly than she can.

Despite the greater knowledge of the poet, therefore, the relationship between poet and speaker is a sympathetic one: there is no tension involved. The bride expresses an emotion which the poet explains by placing it in a context of naturalistic and elemental life, and thus his absence is no more than apparent; for his enveloping presence is as crucial to our perception of the values in this poem as is his direction-pointing in 'Deceptions' or his interpreting voice in 'Next, Please'. Far less easy, and

---

[6] Quoted in D. J. Enright (ed.), *Poets of the 1950s*, The Kenkyusha Press, Tokyo 1955, p. 77. Cf. *Jill*, p. 195, when John Kemp wakes up on the morning of the day that Jill is expected for tea: 'For one curious transient second he thought he knew how a bride feels on the morning of her wedding'.

raising far more problems, 'Poetry of Departures' (p. 34) is teasingly elusive about the credibility of its speaker:

> Sometimes you hear, fifth-hand,
> As epitaph:
> *He chucked up everything*
> *And just cleared off,*
> And always the voice will sound
> Certain you approve . . .

The poem begins with an appeal to us via the second-person pronoun, but this is no more than a pretext for the speaker, who is talking to, and about, himself. His appeal to common sentiments at the beginning of the second stanza does not necessarily bring our assent: we do not *all* hate home; and hardly has he made a somewhat dubious generalization than he begins to reveal some of his attitudes and inadequacies—'detest', for example, is a much more powerful word than 'hate'. Additionally, the growing strength of the verbs draws our attention to the person using them, so that by the middle of the second stanza we are observing the 'I' of the poem with some curiosity.

Is the speaker being exposed? Is Larkin, for poetic purposes, assuming an attitude he wishes to discredit? Or is he directly appealing to us to share and acknowledge this attitude as a familiar one? Most of us share something of this dissatisfaction from time to time, but we generally recognize its tendency to unreality. The poem presents alternative possibilities only as italicized clichés or romantic escapism, and the nub on which it turns is the fact that the thought of 'something else' as a tantalizing possibility is what actually helps the speaker stay 'sober and industrious'. In spite of the speaker's dissatisfaction, the things which he opposes to it are simply not viable possibilities, although he still desires what is exposed as artificial and self-dramatizing. If we decide that the poem's point is that romantic fantasy breeds dissatisfaction in the human imagination, we may be denying the wryness of tone at the end of the poem: 'Books; china; a life/Reprehensibly perfect'. If, on the other hand, we shift our interpretation onto the speaker and decide that the play of his consciousness is the focal-point of the poem, then the poem's manner is more detached, and what is being questioned and exposed is the speaker's view of his own choices. To reduce one's needs and desires to romantic cliché is no better than reducing one's life to a series of material objects. For all of us, self-dissatisfaction can pave the way to unreal possibilities. To accept that we can never be fully satisfied with the result of our choices is to be less deceived than it would be to entertain those possibilities.

The second way of looking at the poem is the more sophisticated and satisfying. It involves the acceptance of a dramatic element in the poem, and it hinges on the acceptance and recognition of a distance between poet and speaker. In such a context, of course, readings may grow erratic, and a critic may create a speaker only to see him run away with the poem. Yet the very act of writing in the first person involves the author turning himself into a character, whose attitude here is an organic part of the poem's action. As the dramatization of an attitude which is simultaneously recognized as familiar and shown up to be inadequate the poem is highly successful; but this reading depends on the admission of a dramatic element by means of which the poet uses a transparent speaker to dramatize attitudes with which he assumes his readers' familiarity. If we deny the dramatic element, then the poem immediately becomes far less demanding and interesting. This may be only a question of emphasis, but to deny the dramatic placement of the speaker is to put 'Poetry of Departures' among the weaker poems in the collection, for the least successful poems in *The Less Deceived* are those which move farthest away from a dramatic context. The hallmark of these poems is an extreme and morbid self-consciousness, which is apparently offered directly and for its own sake, and which is not placed in relation to any wider sense of values or perspective, any more than the speaking voice of the poem is placed or qualified. 'Skin' (p. 43) expresses such self-consciousness through an apparent detachment from self, as the speaker addresses his own skin. As the skin becomes an image of self the poem finds correlatives for an awareness of internal change. Again, however, the predominant feeling is one of loss and unexplained failure (why 'a soiled name'?), which pulls against the recognition of the necessity of growing old as the skin is wryly told: 'You must learn your lines'. Unfortunately this self-conscious play on the central image serves only to highlight the self-consciousness of the poem, and to drive it even further into itself.

The attempt to look into oneself from the perspective of others is taken a stage further in 'If, My Darling' (p. 42):

> If my darling were once to decide
> Not to stop at my eyes,
> But to jump, like Alice, with floating skirt into
>   my head . . .
>
> She would find herself looped with the creep of
>   varying light,
> Monkey-brown, fish-grey, a string of infected circles
> Loitering like bullies, about to coagulate . . .

To take others inside his head is to take them through the looking-glass into a world where all things are inverted and all expectations reversed. The ideas are given entirely as sensory feelings—'claw-footed', 'tantalus', 'creep', 'infected', 'coagulate', 'swill-tub'—and the violence of the language suggests a consciousness of self so intense as to amount to a morbid self-hatred. As James Naremore has said: 'It is difficult to admire the speaker even for his honesty; his confession is so irrational and masochistic that one doubts if he knows himself as well as he thinks'.[7] The tremendous bitterness is self-directed, and hence comes across as destructive rather than revelatory or illuminating, let alone confessional.

Only distance and detachment can protect Larkin's poetry from such damaging introversion. The beneficent effects of distancing are well illustrated in 'Spring' (p. 36) which also centres on the self. The catalogue of visual images in the octave leads up to the speaker, but he too is seen from outside; and although he describes himself as 'an indigestible sterility', we do see him in the context of spring if not actually participating in it. By placing his speaker in the context of ongoing life the poet ensures that the poem is not exclusively self-concentrated. The poem is dominated by self-pity, but this is made the basis for the general statements to which the poem moves, and is also part of a dramatic tension: the speaker expresses both his awareness of the magical rebirth of spring as well as his exclusion from it. By using himself as an example, too, he avoids either getting over-involved in himself, or bogged down in telling us about his 'sterility'. The poem does 'digest' him, for his exclusion affords him a perspective on the unity of human and natural. He may not be part of it, but he recognizes its authenticity; and as (in the octave) people were like fairies or nature-spirits, so (in the sestet) spring is a daughter of earth:

> Spring, of all seasons most gratuitous,
> Is fold of untaught flower, is race of water,
> Is earth's most multiple, excited daughter;
>
> And those she has least use for see her best,
> Their paths grown craven and circuitous,
> Their visions mountain-clear, their needs immodest.

The absence of articles takes up and extends the ritualistic qualities at the beginning of the poem, and the jolt of the final word—a negative which refers to a positive need—wakes us to the intensity of the speaker's feeling. His self-pity and self-consciousness have themselves been placed in

[7] James Naremore, 'Philip Larkin's "Lost World"', *Contemporary Literature*, 15 (1974), p. 343.

perspective, and such control makes for better poetry than the diseased language of 'If, My Darling'. It is important to stress that the distancing here is just as functional as it is in, say, 'Wedding Wind', where speaker and poet are more obviously differentiated. And even if, in 'Spring', Larkin is writing about himself and in his own voice, the self-distancing prevents the over-morbidity of self-appraisal that characterizes 'Age' (p. 30) or 'Skin'.

The poems that are overburdened with self-consciousness in *The Less Deceived* are the weakest because they are too static: they state rather than explore. The better poems, in contrast, reveal the varied means by which Larkin explores human emotion. These generally involve his capacity to create and exploit distancing devices of one kind or another, be they extended metaphors, naturalistic contexts with symbolic overtones, or a dramatic element in the presentation of the speaker. Most effectively and most unobtrusively, Larkin can use a subjective presence whose effect is quite different from that created by the manipulating deity of 'Deceptions', and one of the most distinctive features of his poetry is a capacity to sound conversational (as well as to reproduce conversation). A serious poem may thus have a deceptively casual tone, yet the conversational atmosphere lets the poet orchestrate a low-key meditation which allows for changes of pace and intensity, which in turn keep us alive to the constant play of a thinking mind. The immediacy of such a meditation makes for its drama.

Colloquialism and control blend superbly in 'Lines on a Young Lady's Photograph Album' (p. 13), the colloquialism working ironically against the formal-sounding title. Yet the casualness of the situation (the speaker is looking over a photograph album) should not blind us to the meditation on time and change that takes place in the poem, as the speaker glances over and ponders a series of frozen images from the past. There is a sharp contrast between the movement of his mind and the fixity of what he is looking at, and this contrast is partly realized by the alternating past and present tenses of the poem. Again, therefore, the concentration is visual. The first three stanzas recreate the excitement of the speaker as he looks at the album, an excitement he tries to shrug off with a defensive pun about the men surrounding the girl in one of the photographs: 'Not quite your class, I'd say, dear, on the whole'.[8] The poem then strikes a more

[8] Timms (*Philip Larkin*, p. 77) observes that this poem recreates 'not the photographs, but the experience of looking at the photographs in the presence of the young lady'. Timms rightly stresses the poem's dramatic element, but there is no evidence for the girl's presence: the speaker is half musing, half addressing the album. See also Patricia Ball, 'The Photographic Art', *REL*, 3, No. 2 (1962), pp. 50–8, for brief comments on this poem.

obviously serious note. After musing on the nature of photography the poem considers the effect of the past on the present, or more particularly the effect of someone else's past on *our* present. The question arises whether the greater reality belongs to the photographs or to the girl, and it is clear that, for the speaker, meaning and vitality are condensed in the past and its images. The speculative syntax carries the speaker from excitement to resignation, from his own faltering control of his emotions to his recognition that the girl's poise (beautifully suggested by the image of her 'balanced on a bike against a fence') is both intimidating and unattainable, living as it does for ever in the past.

The rhymes of the first stanza anticipate the entire movement of the speaker's consciousness, reducing 'ages' to 'images' on 'pages'. Fluidity has become fixity. And yet however we may be saddened by the irrevocability of the past, its corresponding attraction is that it makes no demands upon us: 'It leaves us free to cry'. The gap between past and present for the speaker is also the gap between 'I' and 'you', between 'eye' and 'page', and the gap is realized dramatically for the reader in the stanza-break:

> We know *what was*
> Won't call on us to justify
> Our grief, however hard we yowl across
>
> The gap from eye to page. So I am left . . .

The punning proximity of 'eye' and 'I' substantiates that the gap between eye and page is also the gap between 'I' and 'image', between the living speaker and the girl in the photographs stripped of her vitality. Notwithstanding the desperate knowledge that this gap can never be bridged, the speaker does achieve resolution of a sort, even as he laments

> . . . a past that no one now can share,
> No matter whose your future; calm and dry,
> It holds you like a heaven, and you lie
> Unvariably lovely there,
> Smaller and clearer as the years go by.

Although the 'boldness' of Larkin's lover is in question, one cannot but think of Keats:

> Bold Lover, never, never canst thou kiss,
> Though winning near the goal—yet, do not grieve;

<blockquote>
She cannot fade, though thou hast not thy bliss,
For ever wilt thou love, and she be fair!
</blockquote>

Despite their similar thematic focus a major difference between these poems is of course the familiarity of one speaker with his subject and the speculative questioning of the other. Nevertheless the title of Larkin's poem may echo that of Keats's, and the fixity of the figures and the opposition of permanence and fulfilment are crucial similarities.

Nor is Larkin's qualification any less rigorous than that of Keats. To use his own language, the past is 'condensed' into an unreal 'heaven'; a 'bathing' girl has become 'dry', like a flower pressed between the leaves of a book, and the unreality is hammered home by the adjacent rhymes of 'dry' and 'lie'.[9] In so far as it shows us what *was* rather than what *is*, a photograph is always an untruth. Yet in a world of flux and motion we may well yearn for the stability it seems to represent, the stability with which it is all too easy to endow the past. The speaker's tone has developed from excitement to resignation, and at the end of the poem he has no illusions about his exclusion from the girl's future as well as from her past. The yearning for the unvarying loveliness of the girl remains, although the unnaturalness of such loveliness draws attention to itself poetically by the unusual form of the word, which highlights the negative prefix: *un*variable rather than *in*variable. The final line both reminds us that the past becomes clearer in relation to its distance from the present, and suggestively recalls the implicit hint in the title that the speaker's consciousness of his own impending age is now projected onto the album. As the poem ends, therefore, its main image is in front of our eyes as well as in front of the speaker's; but we see him clearly as well. A similar unillusioned regret pervades 'Maiden Name' (p. 23), where the speaker considers a girl's maiden name in relation to her identity as a married woman. Once again, the past is accepted as a haven, but in this poem there is no 'I', only a 'we', and the tone neither develops as dramatically nor fluctuates as extremely as it does in 'Lines on a Young Lady's Photograph Album'. Our sense of the speaker is less pronounced, the tone is more elegiac, the movement quieter. The common factor is thematic: both poems exemplify attitudes to the past. We are asked to share the sadness and exclusion of both speakers. Because a lack of deception characterizes the developing play of consciousness, they remain sympathetic.

[9] Christopher Ricks has drawn attention to Larkin's frequent punning on the word 'lie': see 'Lies', *Critical Inquiry*, 2 (Autumn 1975), pp. 121–42. For evidence of Larkin's early awareness of this pun, see *Jill*, pp. 119, 188.

In contrast, 'Reasons for Attendance' (p. 18) compels a far stronger reaction to its speaker. A brilliant exposé of a rationalization, this poem sharply and incisively penetrates its speaker's defensive self-justifications. The title's relationship to the poem lends dramatic tension to our understanding of the poem, for the speaker is standing outside a dance-hall giving reasons for his refusal to go inside. Nevertheless, there he is watching the dancers, and in spite of his rationalizations the underlying reasons for his attendance do emerge.

The fundamental tension in the poem is between what the speaker thinks and what he senses. Drawing a contrast with the music of the trumpet, he tells us that art is his 'calling'.[10] The self-righteousness of his tone is bolstered by the throwaway defensiveness of 'if you like', and his bogus notion of art as a 'calling', with all its overtones of otherworldliness, is completely overthrown by his sensuously revealing relish of 'The wonderful feel of girls'. As the poem lingers on the phrase with the speaker, the incongruous emphasis calls his assertions into question; and a major source of the power of this poem is its effective undermining through tone and verse-form of the speaker's statements. The first stanza has a self-contained, neutral authority, as well as a syntactical smoothness lacking in the rest of the poem; it is also a single sentence, the only stanza-sentence in the poem. This straightforward description of action and situation in the first stanza is qualified in the second by the choppy and discordant questioning and assertion. The only authentic note in this stanza is struck by 'The wonderful feel of girls', the tone of which effectively answers in advance the question 'what/Is sex?':

> Surely, to think the lion's share
> Of happiness is found by couples—sheer
>
> Inaccuracy as far as I'm concerned.

Not even the combined alliteration and assonance of 'surely', 'share', and 'sheer' can take us comfortably and securely over the vast gap between line and line, between stanza and stanza. At this exact mid-point in the poem, and while the speaker is in the process of making a central point, the verse sheers away into emptiness before lurching into 'Inaccuracy'. And in highlighting that word, of course, the poet makes his own

[10] Timms wrongly notes that 'this is the only occasion on which Larkin mentions the fact that he is a poet in the whole of his mature work' (*Philip Larkin*, p. 87). He overlooks 'I Remember, I Remember', and his absolute equation of poet and speaker is surely over-confident.

judgement on what is being said. Now continuity has disappeared from the poem, and the speaker staggers on uneasily from phrase to phrase. Furthermore, the rhyme has affected the whole tone of the rationalization by sounding a discordant note throughout, for in no stanza have we been consistently allowed the security of full rhymes. The equality of 'here' and 'sheer' in the second stanza leaves no place for 'share', and also emphasizes the gap after 'sheer'. In the first stanza 'happiness' reflects fully neither 'glass' nor 'face' (nor do these reflect each other), and the chiming of 'bell' and 'well' in the third stanza appropriately leaves the 'individual' stranded. Nor are the first and third lines in any of these first three stanzas blessed with full rhymes. But the poem's firm conclusion rests on complete rhymes:

> But not for me, nor I for them; and so
> With happiness. Therefore I stay outside,
> Believing this; and they maul to and fro
> Believing that; and both are satisfied,
> If no one has misjudged himself. Or lied.

By permitting the dominant rhyme of the stanza, and indeed of the poem, to fall with accumulated force on the final word, Larkin causes this rhyme (which surely drowns the 'calling' of art) to reverberate back through the poem. It explodes the speaker's self-deception, and his sudden acknowledgement of the falseness of his rationalization makes explicit what has been apparent all along to the reader. The poet has conclusively exposed his speaker through structure and versification.

The use of a speaker is put to different effect in 'Church Going' (p. 28), Larkin's best-known poem in *The Less Deceived*. When he was asked by Ian Hamilton if he had planned this poem as 'a debate between poet and *persona*', Larkin replied: 'Well, in a way. The poem starts by saying, you don't really know about all this, you don't know what a rood-loft is—why do you come here, why do you bother to stop and look round? The poem is seeking an answer. . . . I think one has to dramatize oneself a little. I don't arse about in churches when I'm alone'.[11] As we would expect from this comment, the most interesting aspect of 'Church Going' is the development of the speaker's attitude; and so unobtrusive is the poet's technique in this respect that by the time we have become involved in the gravity and seriousness of the end of the poem we may have forgotten the casually informal tone of the poem's opening stanzas. As the poem

[11] Ian Hamilton interview, in Graham Martin and P. N. Furbank (eds), *Twentieth Century Poetry*, The Open University Press, Milton Keynes 1975, p. 246.

develops the poet infuses himself into the speaker's radiating concerns, so that his unease and self-consciousness gradually disappear: he attempts less and less to be funny, and the questions he is asking grow in seriousness. From his posited situation of walking around inside a particular church at the beginning of the poem, the speaker has come to make general statements about the human need for spiritual order. The unexpected change of tenses in the third stanza moves the poem away from the dramatic immediacy of the first two, and from 'wondering' (the word is important to the poem) about the future and function of churches the speaker tries to look ahead to the very last person who will 'seek/This place for what it was . . .' It is in this context—the mention of *this* place reminds us that we are still in the church with him—that his thoughts revert specifically to himself at the end of the fifth stanza, no longer with any trace of the uneasiness that characterized his tone at the beginning. The penultimate stanza is organized as a prelude to the final statement, which is surely authoritative. The speaker wonders if the last person to seek the place for what it was will be 'my representative':

> Bored, uninformed, knowing the ghostly silt
> Dispersed, yet tending to this cross of ground
> Through suburb scrub because it held unspilt
> So long and equably what since is found
> Only in separation—marriage, and birth,
> And death, and thoughts of these—for which was built
> This special shell?

The poem begins its movement to solemn statement by answering the question at the end of this stanza: as Larkin said, the poem *is* seeking an answer, and it is no longer just an answer for the speaker. In the next (and final) stanza the tenses return to the present, and the first person pronouns, singular and plural, give way to the general 'someone'. It is only because the poet comes to answer the speaker at the end that the poem can bear the weight of such generalization in answer to the speaker's 'wondering', for the poet articulates the need for something serious with more gravity than the speaker has shown in the course of the poem. Likewise the inverted word-order at the beginning of the last stanza leaves colloquialism behind, and ushers in the note of solemnity on which Larkin wishes the poem to conclude.

'Compulsion', 'destiny', 'hunger', 'gravitation': the language mingles the human with something beyond humanity, but something that Larkin will not accept as religious. He has insisted that 'Church Going' is 'entirely secular'. Going to church, in this poem, has to do with communal humanity or, as Larkin has put it, 'the union of the important stages of human life'.[12] The poem is concerned with felt needs rather than with belief, and because those needs have to be shown to be felt, the subject-matter of the poem cannot be detached from the workings of the speaker's mind. The play of his consciousness, controlled by the poet who himself intrudes directly at the end, is the force governing the poem's effectiveness.[13]

In relation to the rest of the collection, 'Church Going' is a poem about learning rather than about being 'undeceived'. The speaker is struggling towards knowledge rather than working his way out of illusion. The reader shares both his journey and his encounter with the poet at the end of the poem, and it is our sense of having to some extent shared the speaker's struggle that renders the voice at the end authoritative. Indeed, at the end of this poem an authoritative presence is established more overtly than in any other poem in *The Less Deceived*; and it is certainly true that the most striking aspect of the collection is the variety of ways in which such a presence is established at the centre of most poems. I wish finally to look at two poems whose methods in this respect are almost completely opposed: 'I Remember, I Remember' and 'At Grass'.

Whereas 'At Grass' aims at a degree of impersonality, 'I Remember, I Remember' (p. 38) creates the illusion of being intimately personal, while at the same time showing just how far Larkin is from being anything like a confessional poet. Larkin was born at Coventry, and of course writes poetry, but we should be wary of equating speaker and poet in this poem. In any case, any such equation is of little help; for although the speaker may well be a version of Larkin he is mainly concerned with telling us not what did happen to him, but what did *not* happen. The point of the poem is general rather than personal. What is remembered, therefore, is a series of representative non-happenings, and one of the most apparently personal poems becomes one of the least personal. The poem sets out to destroy the literary and celluloid mythologizing of adolescence. Thus the allusion in the title to Thomas Hood's famous sentimentalization of childhood remembrance is viciously ironic, for the poem ruthlessly demolishes any such idealizing nostalgia.

We have to accept the situation we are given at the beginning of the poem as simultaneously literal and metaphorical: 'Coming up England by a different line/For once, early in the cold new year', the speaker looks

[12] Ian Hamilton interview.
[13] For a detailed commentary on this poem, see R. N. Parkinson, '"To Keep our Metaphysics Warm": A Study of "Church Going" by Philip Larkin', *The Critical Survey*, 5 (Winter 1971), pp. 224–33.

at his past from an unusual perspective, and it seems both new and unfamiliar to him. Negatives are brutally hurled against the mythic stereotypes, which are in tatters by the end of the poem. The presence of a friend involves the reader in the poem. Only in the first and last stanzas does the speaker say anything aloud: the bulk of the poem is an interior monologue; and although the friend has not shared the speaker's musing (as we have), his comment at the end—'You look as if you wished the place in Hell'—is what our response might be. Thus he becomes a version of the reader. Moreover, his question is dramatically appropriate to the poem's completeness. Not only does it formulate the reader's response; it also gives the speaker a chance to come out of himself, to detach himself from his own vehement demythologizing, and to comment generally (in the line detached from the rest of the poem): 'Nothing, like something, happens anywhere'. Growing out of the preceding context of relentless destruction, this most general of generalizations allows a poem of great emotional violence to end on a note of detachment and calm. It is crucial to the balance of the poem that the speaker, in refusing to be deceived about his childhood, should also refuse to go to the other extreme and bemoan its ordinariness.

Additionally, this final line grows out of and completes the form of the poem. Standing alone after the seventh five-line stanza, this line would seem to be on its own, and emphasized for isolation. But this poem is concerned with yet a further variety of deception; and in addition its form and technique are also deceptive. The rhyme-scheme does not coalesce with the stanzaic organization.[14] The rhyme is divided into units of nine lines, thus: abccbaabc. Seven stanzas (thirty-five lines) and four units of rhyme (thirty-six lines) necessitate an additional line following the last stanza to complete the rhyming pattern of the poem. As well as completing the speaker's meditation and detaching his general conclusion from the violent negation of the bulk of the poem, therefore, the final line also fulfils the poem's formal shape. Another significant aspect of the rhyme is that each nine-line unit has three sounds, which means that each sound has two rhyming partners. We thus come at each rhyme by two different lines. And because many of the rhyme words are well-distanced from each other, the poem sets up a pattern of echo as well as rhyme, which has an obvious dramatic function in a poem about the distorted messages we may get from our own memory. In many ways 'I Remember, I Remember' is not what it seems. Its completeness and

---

[14] Timms draws attention to the way the rhyme-scheme breaks across the stanza-form: *Philip Larkin*, p. 81.

pattern are not immediately perceptible, but it deceives only to surprise, and its point is very clearly made by its form.

The poet stands behind the speaker, manipulating the form of the meditation, weaving a pattern to contain the extreme negative emphases required by the poem. The result is hard-headed rather than self-demolishing, for the low-key ending qualifies and softens the negative and necessary violence of the anti-sentimentalization. The poem's authority is thus established by the relationship between its technical features and what is said by the speaker.

In 'At Grass' (p. 45) a speaking 'I' is replaced by 'the eye', and from this opening word the poem's manipulative focus is visual. The effect is akin to that of seeing a film and simultaneously hearing a commentary on it (the poem was written after Larkin had seen a film of racehorses in retirement), and while the commentator has certainly responded to the sights he is presenting, his emotions are dissolved in his description of the scene. The first stanza tells us, in the present tense, what the 'eye' can see. The second stanza moves into the past tense, as it speculates on the racehorses' lives, and everything is presented for us to *see*. The words 'distances', 'faint', 'artificed', 'inlay', and 'faded' appeal to the visual imagination in order to hint at the frailty, the fragility, the precariousness of all things human; and these qualities are reinforced by 'fable'. As we are led quickly into the next stanza, an immediate change of rhythm brings the past vividly to life in the present:

> Silks at the start: against the sky
> Numbers and parasols: outside,
> Squadrons of empty cars, and heat,
> And littered grass: then the long cry
> Hanging unhushed till it subside
> To stop-press columns on the street.

This stanza contains no main verb: it is of course a continuation of the sentence begun in the previous stanza, and the past is here recreated by a further intensification of the visual details corroborated by the broken rhythm. Then the rhythm evens out to imitate 'the long cry' described, while the visual impressions, preserved in 'hanging' and 'subside', come to rest on 'stop-press columns'.

The final stanzas recall us to the present tense and scene:

> Do memories plague their ears like flies?
> They shake their heads. Dusk brims the shadows.

Summer by summer all stole away,
The starting-gates, the crowds and cries—
All but the unmolesting meadows.
Almanacked, their names live . . .

Martin Scofield has acutely observed that here 'the poet himself has almost completely disappeared, and the poem is almost completely absorbed in the life it is describing, while still maintaining for important reasons of fidelity the sense of an observer'.[15] The poet's obvious feeling for the horses is suggested by their gestures' apparent answer to his questions, but his strongest point of sympathetic identification is his fascination with their lack of identity—a fascination hinted at in the 'anonymous' of the first stanza and brought out most strongly at the end of the poem. One of Larkin's notes on the worksheets of the poem reads: 'magic of names—names woven into human world [. . . then] horses, free at last, become horses'.[16] The horses have escaped the fictions imposed on them as symbols of human aspiration, and have become representations of unconscious identity. Liberated from the past and from the demands of time, they have finally become themselves in a pastoral world of innocence and permanence.

These horses are in no sense symbolic. Although the poem lingers on them it is the poet's attitude which endows them with significance. Their shedding of identity is seen as freedom, a desire for which is expressed in other poems in *The Less Deceived* as a death-wish. Death, after all, is the ultimate and absolute liberation from identity,[17] and a growing fascination with death informs Larkin's subsequent poetry. The unity of the poems in this book, which may seem to be belied by their diversity of manner, can be traced to a hard core of thematic concerns: the human sense of identity, the images of the past and the illusions of the future that we cherish and distort, our unawareness of the essential seriousness of so much of what we do. We are rarely in any doubt as to what Larkin's metaphors mean, because the authorial voice often functions as a commentary explaining them for us; and the elusiveness of such poems as 'Dry-Point' and 'Absences' suggests the dangers (for this poet) of abandoning his authority and trying to write like a symbolist.

So much of what happens in the poems is both shown and explained to us, and it is essential to stress yet again the visual aspects of Larkin's

[15] Martin Scofield, 'The Poetry of Philip Larkin', *Massachusetts Review*, 17 (1976), p. 380.
[16] Worksheets of 'At Grass', reprinted in the Larkin issue of *Phoenix*, pp. 91–102.
[17] Cf. 'Wants', p. 22.

poetry. These take various forms. They are most obviously apparent when we are presented with a central visual image and a commentary upon it, as in 'Next, Please' or 'No Road'. They are apparent also in the cinematic re-creation of images in 'At Grass', or in Larkin's rendering of the girl's realization of her ruin in 'Deceptions', where the illumination of what has happened breaks into her mind as 'light'. More important even than these, however, are the visual demands that Larkin's technique makes of us: the formal reflections of the first reflective stanza of 'Triple Time'; the experience of examining a photograph album re-enacted for us in our relationship to the printed page; the necessary visual perception by the reader of the enclosing rhymes of 'Wires' and the complex rhyme-scheme of 'I Remember, I Remember' (a timely reminder that rhymes are seen as well as heard); and the exposure of the speaker of 'Reasons for Attendance' by line-ending and stanza-break—not forgetting, of course, that we see him 'drawn' against the lighted glass in all his transparency.

Such technical manipulation establishes poetic authority. The unhealthy and unhelpful self-consciousness of some poems is more than redeemed by the sophisticated detachment of others, whereby the poet establishes an authoritative centre for the poems by the implicit method of using a speaker whose credibility varies from poem to poem. The formal devices of the poems can be used to qualify the speakers' statements and judgements, with the poet himself submerged in the technique. It is not fanciful, I think, to suggest that the attractiveness of the horses in 'At Grass' is partly an attraction that Larkin the poet feels for abandoning his identity. As poems in *The Less Deceived* begin talking about 'someone' or 'no one' we can sense them moving into a void,[18] a void which deepens in Larkin's next volume. For *The Whitsun Weddings* is distinguished by the increasing subtlety of the stances adopted by the poet.

---

[18] See, for example, of the poems discussed in this chapter, 'Lines on a Young Lady's Photograph Album', 'Maiden Name', 'Church Going', 'Reasons for Attendance'. The same point can be made in relation to often-confusing modulation in the use of pronouns in many other poems.

III

The Whitsun Weddings

The masks of *The Whitsun Weddings* are more subtle and varied than those of Larkin's previous poetry. Greater control and more absolute detachment increase the general range of the book as well as the impact of particular poems. Notwithstanding the general accessibility of subject-matter, however, the manner has often proved elusive, especially in poems where a speaker is being used. This is not, I hope, to create complexities where none exist, and it might therefore be as well to open the discussion by looking at a poem which Larkin has described as his least understood. 'Naturally the Foundation will Bear Your Expenses' (p. 13) does many things which it may not initially seem to do. For this reason, and also because it is the most obvious example in *The Whitsun Weddings* of Larkin's use of a speaker, the poem provides a convenient introduction to the collection.

The poem manages to be at once hilariously funny, bitterly satirical, and deeply serious. Larkin's rigorous judgement on the speaker is contained and directed by the form: the jaunty rhythm and reassuringly predictable rhyme (especially the audacious bisyllabic rhymes) work together to expose the speaker's lack of essential seriousness:

> Hurrying to catch my Comet
>   One dark November day,
> Which soon would snatch me from it
>   To the sunshine of Bombay,
> I pondered pages Berkeley
>   Not three weeks since had heard,
> Perceiving Chatto darkly
>   Through the mirror of the Third.

The paper given in California three weeks ago is to be given again in Bombay, broadcast on the BBC Third programme, and possibly published by Chatto and Windus. This particular jet-setting academic is clearly intent on publishing rather than perishing, and here he is mercilessly exposed in full flight. On his recording of *The Whitsun Weddings* Larkin has bemoaned the labelling of this poem as 'light verse', and it should be stressed that, as the measure of the poet's detachment from the speaker, the humour is paradoxically an indication of the poem's seriousness. Larkin has said that the poem is as serious as anything he has written: 'Certainly it was a dig at the middleman who gives lots of talks to America and then brushes them up and does them on the Third and then brushes them up again and puts them out as a book with Chatto. Why he should be blamed for not sympathizing with the crowds on Armistice Day, I don't quite know.... I've never written a poem that has been less understood'.[1] The contrasts of the poem set the academic hocus-pocus and name-dropping of the 'intellectual' world against a ritualistic commemoration that is of enduring significance to crowds of ordinary people. The speaker's description of the Armistice Day service as 'solemn-sinister wreath-rubbish' and as a nursery game allows us to assume the value the poet places on the service, and although the value is not specifically explained or analysed in any detail, we still draw our own conclusions about the speaker; for the poem is affirming the importance of those very things the speaker cannot understand or appreciate. As so often happens in Larkin's poems, too, the changing tenses (from past to present at the end of the poem) serve to change our perspective on the speaker, and finally we see him close-up, in all the immediacy of his self-involvement, leaving behind the things he has so scathingly criticized. His delusions about his own maturity, nicely pointed by his reference to nursery games and to England's need to grow up, are surely corroborated by his twisted allusion to St Paul's first Epistle to the Corinthians at the end of the first verse. He may well want to display his knowledge, too, hence his use of the classical name for the south wind ('Auster') to tell us that he is travelling south. And the mention of E. M. Forster is not only a typical instance of academic name-dropping (replacing the familiar initials with the unfamiliar christian name is a superb touch); it recalls

[1] Ian Hamilton interview, in Graham Martin and P. N. Furbank (eds), *Twentieth Century Poetry*, The Open University Press, Milton Keynes 1975, pp. 248–9. John Wain has argued for this poem as an example of deeply felt satiric poetry: see his 'Engagement or Withdrawal? Some Notes on the Work of Philip Larkin', *Critical Quarterly*, 6(1964), pp. 171–2. See also Harry Chambers, 'Some Light Views of a Serious Poem: a footnote to the misreading of Philip Larkin's "Naturally the Foundation will Bear Your Expenses"', Larkin issue of *Phoenix*, 11/12, pp. 110–14.

to the reader a wholly different passage to India and reminds us of a writer who, in *Howards End* as well as in *A Passage to India*, seriously attempted to evaluate English culture. The most telling contrast in the poem is between the subsidized academic, whose expenses (for *my* Comet and *my* taxi) are naturally being borne by the foundation, and 'crowds' paying respects to those who gave their lives for their country. The difference is not only between paying and being paid. It also involves contrasting value systems between which there is no relationship, and there is no doubt where Larkin's sympathies lie.

By bringing us around to a reconsideration of its title, therefore, this poem leaves the speaker with no credibility whatever. The title of 'A Study of Reading Habits' (p. 31) has a detached and analytic quality which puts it in ambivalent relationship to the poem, and which serves again to differentiate poet and speaker. Larkin uses the speaker's reflection on his reading habits to illustrate dramatically the illusions and fantasies fostered by pulp fiction. False expectation and wish-fulfilment are all he has got from books. Having identified wholly with what he has read and having lived a vicarious imaginative life of sex and violence he is left only with his own inadequacy, recognition of which forces him finally to snarl: 'Get stewed: / Books are a load of crap'. The speaker cannot find reasons for his sense of inadequacy any more than the academic on his way to Bombay can see the limitations of his own self-satisfaction, but in each case the speaker is used to focus important concerns of whose full significance he is unaware.

The speaker of 'Wild Oats' (p. 41)—a title also arousing expectations which the poem proceeds to turn upside-down—has greater self-knowledge, but his wryly self-deprecating story is fearfully defensive:

> About twenty years ago
> Two girls came in where I worked—
> A bosomy English rose
> And her friend in specs I could talk to.

As the poem develops it gradually reveals his obsession with the 'bosomy English rose', although, as he says, 'it was the friend I took out'. Anyone obsessed with a girl he did not take out twenty years ago deserves our pity, to say the least, but the speaker is careful to shield his feelings. He tells us a lot of facts, although the discordant rhymes (the only full rhyme is the last one of the poem) comment on him by echoing the disharmony behind his factual barrage. The account he presents of his experience relies almost entirely on statistics: twenty years, two girls, seven years, four hundred letters, one ring costing ten guineas, numerous cathedral cities, about five rehearsals. At once ironical and self-mocking, this list is mainly designed to cover pain, as well as to give us the facts, and even his attempt at a joke is self-defensive at the same time as it points to the failure of the relationship to come to anything: 'Unknown to the clergy'. All the facts added up to was an agreement that he was selfish and withdrawn—hardly useful knowledge, as his ironical tone suggests—and the two girls of the beginning of the poem have been finally reduced to two photographs of the girl he did not take out. Anything less like the sowing of wild oats would be hard to imagine, and the poem's pained bewilderment marshals the feelings of a man who is permanently out of date.

Taken together, these three poems adduce a shifting relationship between poet and speaker which makes varying demands of the reader. We have moved from the poet's scathing judgement on the academic of 'Naturally the Foundation will Bear Your Expenses', to the dramatic illustration of the effects of certain reading habits, to the sympathetic presentation of a sad account of failed relationships. To appreciate these variations in the poet-speaker relationship may help us understand J. R. Watson's contention that 'the poet whom Larkin most closely represents is Browning'.[2] Yet Watson's discussion of 'Mr Bleaney' (p. 10) and his interpretation of the poem as a condemnation of 'Bleaney's desacrilized existence'[3] weaken the force of his point: by concentrating on the apparent inadequacies of Mr Bleaney himself Watson completely ignores the question of the speaker's function in this poem. As Timms has pointed out, 'the speaker is an intellectual, and Bleaney was not',[4] and this difference, or rather the speaker's sense of it, is essential to the poem. Bleaney does not speak for himself, of course, and the main focus of the poem is neither Mr Bleaney nor what his landlady has to say about Mr Bleaney, but the speaker's response to what she says. He measures the difference between himself and the room's previous occupant.

In the first two stanzas the speaker's perceptions of his surroundings are interplayed with the sound of his landlady's voice. The next three stanzas recount what the speaker learns from his landlady about Mr Bleaney—his daily habits, his food preferences, the system by which he played the soccer pools, and the 'yearly frame' of his life. At the beginning of the penultimate stanza the conjunctive 'But' changes the

[2] Watson, 'The Other Larkin', *Critical Quarterly*, 17(1975), p. 348.
[3] Ibid, p. 352.
[4] David Timms, *Philip Larkin,* Oliver and Boyd, Edinburgh 1973, p. 97.

whole direction of the poem as the speaker wonders how Bleaney felt about living alone in a room like this:

> But if he stood and watched the frigid wind
> Tousling the clouds, lay on the fusty bed
> Telling himself that this was home, and grinned,
> And shivered, without shaking off the dread
>
> That how we live measures our own nature,
> And at his age having no more to show
> Than one hired box should make him pretty sure
> He warranted no better, I don't know.

There is nothing whatever in the poem to suggest that Bleaney ever did think along such lines, although the speaker clearly does. Bleaney was apparently content with an existence that cannot satisfy him, and Bleaney thus functions in the poem as a contrasting focus for the speaker's dissatisfaction. Moreover the subject-clause of this long final sentence is suspended until the very end, so that the whole weight of the poem bears down on the speaker's uncertainty: 'I don't know'. The potent absence of Bleaney now ensures that the exclusion is all the speaker's, for although he may not know about Bleaney he surely does know that these things are true for himself. Bleaney was not tormented by his own nature, and for the speaker Bleaney becomes a symbol of all that he himself is not, and comes to stand for the order that his life lacks: thus 'their yearly frame' refers to the yearly frame of Bleaney's daily 'habits', and the flesh and blood person has become, to the mind of the speaker, an abstract personification of habits within an ordered framework. Mr Bleaney's life[5] has had a structure undisturbed by the speaker's self-consciousness, and it is in no way to the latter's advantage that his perceptions about his own life are more penetrating than any that may have been entertained by his predecessor. The external details of Bleaney's life suggest interest—in the garden, for example—and a routine that, for him, served adequately to organize his existence. The only thing keeping the speaker from envy is his realization that Mr Bleaney's way of life is not for him.

   This poem therefore presents us with the speaker's feelings of exclusion, but the degree of sympathy with which we may respond to these is extremely hard to gauge. How, exactly, do we respond to his dread 'That how we live measures our own nature'? This statement is emphasized by

[5] It is hinted, in 'the Bodies', 'one hired box', and the sinister 'They moved him', that Mr Bleaney may be dead.

its position at the beginning of a stanza, and it may well be questionable. On one level it is unexceptionable: of course our lives manifest our own nature. But what sort of judgement is implied in 'measure'? And do we assent to the statement in the materialistic sense in which the speaker is using it? We can see and understand his 'dread', although we may still feel it to be mistaken. Larkin refuses to give us an answer here, and we are thus left pondering the speaker's dread. But it is important that we do not allow ourselves unthinkingly and uncritically to absorb such momentous generalizations, which may be working in the poem to comment on the speaker.

'Dockery and Son' (p. 37) raises similar problems. Again, the speaker muses on the difference he feels between himself and another man whom he is not sure he can even remember, but who is now dead. Like 'I Remember, I Remember' from *The Less Deceived*, 'Dockery and Son' tempts us to equate Larkin with his speaker, for both poet and speaker would have been twenty-one in 1943. Again, however, the temptation is futile. As the earlier poem told us what had *not* happened in the speaker's childhood, so this speaker tells us about the 'nothing' he has got, in contrast to Dockery who must have 'got' his son when he was nineteen or twenty. Once again, too, we are prevented from identifying fully with the speaker: the poem opens with someone speaking who is very much a minor character; the speaker falls asleep in the middle of his own poem; and the changing tenses of the first three stanzas do not make it easy to settle down into a firm relationship with him.

The poem's puzzlement revolves around the opposite poles of chance and choice, with a determinism akin to that perceived by Katherine Lind hovering in the background: 'she had believed for a long time that a person's life is directed mainly by their actions, and these in turn are directed by their personality, which is not self-chosen in the first place and modifies itself quite independently of their wishes afterwards'.[6] Beginning with a specific situation—a visit to the funeral of a former university colleague—and opening, like 'Mr Bleaney', with a third person speaking, the poem soon establishes the speaker's feeling of the difference between Dockery and himself; and this developing awareness gives the poem its dramatic dimension.

The poem develops from conversation through a rendering of sense-impressions to internal meditation. It gains depth and power by the easy incorporation of symbolic associations into the informality of its context, and also by the use of naturalistic detail (such as a locked door) to create

[6] *A Girl in Winter*, p. 185.

the predominant mood of isolation before it is overtly mentioned. And, of course, the naturalistic locked door near the beginning anticipates the symbolic doors later in the poem. What the poem is saying is that the beliefs we hold about how to live our lives are not beliefs at all, but assumptions, and innate ones at that. Our lack of knowledge about the inner lives of others or about the reasons for the decisions made by others is thus matched by a corresponding lack of knowledge about all the factors informing our own decisions. The on-going internal drama and the difficulty of finding an answer to the problems it uncovers are matched by the poem's rhyming pattern. As the speaker gropes hesitantly towards a solution, the poet expands the distance between his rhyme words:

> To have no son, no wife,
> No house or land still seemed quite natural.
> Only a numbness registered the shock
> Of finding out how much had gone of life,
> How widely from the others. Dockery, now:
> Only nineteen, he must have taken stock
> Of what he wanted, and been capable
> Of . . . No that's not the difference: rather, how

> Convinced he was he should be added to!

Timms wrongly says that the rhyme-scheme is 'straightforward';[7] it is in fact highly complex. Every stanza has eight lines and four rhymes, but not until the two final stanzas is the rhyming pattern of one stanza repeated in another. The stanza quoted above (the fourth) is the least regular in the poem, in that here the rhyme words are furthest removed from their partners; and of course it is in this stanza that the speaker is most aware of the difference between Dockery and himself. The rhyming pattern of the stanza (abcadcbd) keeps the rhymes at least three lines apart, with two additional sounds between them. The final line of this stanza falters before gathering momentum, and as we move into the next stanza the speaker's gathering conviction is supported by the adjacent rhymes of 'increase'/'these', 'style'/'while'. Still questioning but no longer quite so conversational, the poem hardens into a sense of differences resolved, and as the speaker finds common ground between Dockery and himself the rhyme is regularized so that the final two stanzas share the same rhyming pattern. Resolution and acceptance characterize both rhyme and meditation. They have come about because the speaker no longer feels that there is any difference between himself and Dockery:

[7] Timms, *Philip Larkin*, p. 101.

Life is first boredom, then fear.
Whether or not we use it, it goes,
And leaves what something hidden from us chose,
And age, and then the only end of age.

What the speaker saw, at the beginning of the penultimate stanza, as Dockery's conviction—the word 'convinced' is strategically placed at the beginning of a stanza and, fortuitously, at the beginning of a page—has become his own conviction. Their apparent differences are dissipated by the pronoun 'we', which in turn tries to draw the reader into the final bleak statements.

Whereas 'Mr Bleaney' left us pondering the speaker's awareness of his own emptiness, 'Dockery and Son' draws us into the speaker's mind and then presents a general observation on 'life' for our contemplation. Again, however, we are still observing the speaker. The dramatic impetus of the opening stanzas also informs the conclusion of the poem, and although the poem has moved from a concrete, particularized situation to abstraction and generalization, from a point in time to something offered as a timeless statement, it remains dramatic at the end. We may feel disinclined to accept these final statements as any more than partial truths, which is only to say that the dramatic dimension has shifted: the speaker's perspective on Dockery has been replaced, at the end of the poem, by the reader's perspective on the speaker. Once we have become aware of it, the careful and complex manipulation of rhyme preserves and maintains the dramatic framework of the poem; and it is truly amazing that such technical intricacy should in no way disrupt the conversational tone of the poem. Thus the two final stanzas have to be judged in relation to what precedes them. We are left with the expression of a mood rather than with authoritative statement. However we judge the generalizations here, they express a poignant loneliness.

Larkin explores feelings of isolation or exclusion from many different vantage-points in this book. The extent to which we are all potential prisoners of self is suggested in 'Self's the Man' (p. 24). The speaker contrasts his own life with that of 'Arnold':

Oh, no one can deny
That Arnold is less selfish than I.
He married a woman to stop her getting away
Now she's there all day . . .

The ugly sarcasm, and the note of 'it serves him right', alert us immediately to the fact that something is wrong, and draw our attention to the speaker rather than to Arnold. The apparently confessional but actually complacent 'To compare his life and mine/Makes me feel a swine' likewise rings hollow. Contemptuous of both Arnold and his wife, the speaker needs to see Arnold as a henpecked husband who finally got what he deserved: although his marriage may have been a mistake, 'He still did it for his own sake.' And for the speaker, the difference between Arnold and himself is mainly a question of self-knowledge and self-sufficiency:

> Only I'm a better hand
> At knowing what I can stand
> Without them sending a van—
> Or I suppose I can.

The last line makes explicit that the poem has been no more than a whole series of suppositions about Arnold. For all we know, Arnold could be blissfully happy: any information coming from a mind like that of the speaker is suspect. His genuine lack of self-assurance, which is made obvious in the last line, has been betrayed throughout the poem by the abrupt syntax, the choppily adjacent rhymes, and the skittish movement from point to point. The resentful tone of a man snapping in frustration tells us more about the person employing it than it does about Arnold and his marriage. The speaker finds his view of Arnold satisfying because it enables him to feel superior.

Self may be the man, but self is never enough, as this poem suggests. The obsessive concern with self noted as the most negative feature of *The Less Deceived* is here given a broader dimension: there is 'more turning outward in the poems of *The Whitsun Weddings*'.[8] To some extent the proliferation of masks is an important feature of this 'turning outward'. Each of the five poems discussed so far uses a speaker with whom we are not expected to identify fully and on whom we are forced to make some judgement. The book has given us several personalities; and, as has already been pointed out, it is very important to note that we enter 'Mr Bleaney' and 'Dockery and Son' through the speech of a minor actor in the poem's drama which ensures that, although the consciousness of the speaker is the main consideration, we remain detached observers of it rather than participants. The concluding generalizations are to be contemplated rather than accepted. In these two poems, as in 'Self's the Man', we see the speaker considering himself in relation to another person, with the result that his self-consciousness is presented in a context

[8] Timms, *Philip Larkin*, p. 95.

of relationship rather than on its own. At the centre of this consideration lies a paradox: solitude compels us to try to reach out to the lives of others, but the lives of others remind us of our own solitude. Our most apparently intimate moments are those in which our isolation is most keenly felt. The point is made most forcefully in 'Talking in Bed' (p. 29):

> Talking in bed ought to be easiest,
> Lying together there goes back so far,
> An emblem of two people being honest.

The visual images of the second and third stanzas evoke silence as well as isolation, and indeed the poem is more concerned with silence than with talking. The participles with which the first two lines begin, 'talking' and 'lying', immediately strike a relationship as uneasy as that on the bed, and the pun on 'lying' lends additional force to the rhyme linking the first and third lines, 'easiest'/'honest'. Honesty is not always the easiest policy, a point further emphasized by the echoing 'unrest' of the second stanza.

The opening of this poem draws for us an emblem which is not what it seems to be. The illusion of closeness is dispelled by the language of distance—'far', 'horizon', 'isolation'; and the phrase 'distance from isolation' is qualified by a word of singleness, 'unique', so that the entire phrase suggests even greater isolation, and singleness rather than togetherness. Negatives accumulate as the poem progresses: even '*un*rest' is '*in*complete'. The qualifications of the final stanza, their heavily negative stress reinforced by the triplet rhyme, unobtrusively blend the words 'true' and 'kind' into their exact opposites; and the recollection of the pun on 'lying' brings the poem around to the emblem with which it began, but seen now in an altogether different light. What we might imagine to be a situation of intimate ease has been reversed to one of uneasy distance.

Furthermore, the poem's substance is crucially underpinned by its method; for in contrast to the poems discussed earlier, the personality of the speaker does not intrude on the poem at all. The speaker's suggested personal involvement in the situation he describes works against his detached and impersonal manner, a manner essential to the undermining of intimacy which takes place in the poem. Impossible to locate precisely, the speaker is both in and out of the poem, in the bed and interpreting the emblem for us. And who is 'us'? Its implicit use as a form of address could be directed either at the speaker's lover, or at the reader, in which case it draws the reader into the poem (if not into the bed). So easily does the poem modulate between specific situation and general statement that it is by no means clear exactly where the poem comes from. The particular situation is turned into a generalized emblem of human loneliness, into which we are drawn.

This emblematic impersonality is taken a stage further in 'Faith Healing' (p. 15), which uses the idea of faith healing as a central metaphor for human attitudes to love:

> In everyone there sleeps
> A sense of life lived according to love.
> To some it means the difference they could make
> By loving others, but across most it sweeps
> As all they might have done had they been loved.

This statement has the authority of uncompromising absoluteness. It is one of Larkin's few generalizations offered without qualification. To most people love is something taken rather than given, and taken to compensate for the difference between their expectations of life and the answers with which life has met those expectations. The poem then presents the agonizing self-realization of those who come to learn that their faith cannot heal them, as the stanza continues:

> That nothing cures. An immense slackening ache,
> As when, thawing, the rigid landscape weeps,
> Spreads slowly through them—that, and the voice above
> Saying *Dear child*, and all time has disproved.

The poem reverses its metaphor of faith healing, and the cruellest twist for the sufferers becomes the most unexpected for the reader: as delusions collapse all that is healed is misplaced faith. The inversion of 'that nothing cures' is heavy with ambiguity, capable of meaning both 'that cures nothing' and 'nothing cures that'; such misplaced nostalgic awareness is both powerless and chronically incurable. The sufferers are cured only of their belief that cure was possible, and the final rhyme inexorably matches 'loved' against the negative 'disproved'. The poem's religious dimension suggests also that the need for love reflects a hope of salvation. The responses to the faith healer are given in purely physical terms, the animal-like reactions of the women showing how deeply their need is felt:

> . . . some
> Sheepishly stray, not back into their lives
> Just yet; but some stay stiff, twitching and loud

With deep hoarse tears, as if a kind of dumb
And idiot child within them still survives
To re-awake at kindness, thinking a voice
At last calls them alone, that hands have come
To lift and lighten; and such joy arrives
Their thick tongues blort, their eyes squeeze grief, a crowd
Of huge unheard answers jam and rejoice— . . .

The need is for ultimate recognition of the self: they each believe that the voice is for them alone. That religion used to supply this need, but does so no longer, supports the usefulness and value of the poem's metaphor.

The cumulative effect of the enjambment of the second stanza, where none of the lines is end-stopped, is the building-up of pressure which dramatically recreates the women's intensely passionate need. The poetic detachment gives us the experience in three stages: first we have an external description of the faith healer at work, based on a film Larkin saw of a faith healer; then we are given an insight into the minds of the women; and finally the poet comments in general but powerful terms. Drawing out and setting forth all that has been implicit in the two preceding stanzas, the commentary makes the meaning overt and explicit; and the orchestration of the similar-sounding rhymes 'love'/'above', 'loved'/'disproved', firmly denies the longed-for transcendence. The impersonality of presentation is greater than in 'Talking in Bed', where the visual images were perceived by the speaker from his situation inside the poem, yet both poems move easily between general statement and particular illustration, and much of their appeal is strongly visual. All these things are true of 'Home is so Sad' (p. 17), which employs its visual images to focus a general sense of dislocation between past and present, and between presence and absence. The poem begins with a general statement, and concludes with its visual perceptions and an appeal to the reader:

> You can see how it was:
> Look at the pictures and the cutlery.
> The music in the piano stool. That vase.

'Home' is both a physical reality and an emotional state, and is simultaneously remembered and perceived. What could so easily be subjective and even sentimental—someone talking about home—is here generalized, but generalized by particular visual glimpses through which the experience is made accessible to us. The reader here could of course be a visitor, but it is impossible to read the poem without thinking of our own home. Home, here, is anyone's home.

This poem, like 'Faith Healing', represents a refinement of the technique of metaphor and commentary used extensively throughout *The Less Deceived*. The technique is developed considerably in *The Whitsun Weddings*. There are fewer imaginary symbols, such as the ships of 'Next, Please', and more familiar, naturalistic ones. Many poems are firmly grounded in the realities of the urban world, and as such display Larkin's capacity 'to see things symbolically and not only as part of the modern landscape'.[9] Because Larkin can assume our familiarity with the symbolic properties he uses, their suggestiveness can be exploited more fruitfully than that of an imaginary symbol which requires explanation. He can take more for granted.

Ambulances are a common enough feature of the urban scene, but as they flash past us on their way to someone else's disaster we hardly stop to consider the implications of the chilling impersonality they represent. Larkin's poem 'Ambulances' (p. 33) is compelling precisely because it does consider these implications, and in doing so it causes us to think more deeply about an everyday occurrence. By reminding us of our mortality, ambulances arouse our deepest dreads and fears. This poem is not so much about ambulances as about the human response to them which, usually so fleeting, is here slowed down and dissected by the device of showing us a series of visual frames and then commenting on them:

> Closed like confessionals, they thread
> Loud noons of cities, giving back
> None of the glances they absorb.
> Light glossy grey, arms on a plaque,
> They come to rest at any kerb:
> All streets in time are visited.

The certainty of death underlines the entire poem, and in addition to the precariousness of human life we are reminded of its isolation by the enclosing pattern of the poem's rhyme. A feeling of menace pervades the whole, as apparently random visits to 'any kerb' weave themselves into a sinister pattern of inevitability: 'All streets in time are visited'. And the

---

[9] Colin Falck, 'Philip Larkin' in Martin and Furbank (eds), *Twentieth Century Poetry*, p. 410. Originally entitled 'Essential Beauty', this essay first appeared as a review of *The Whitsun Weddings* in Ian Hamilton's magazine, *The Review*, No. 14, pp. 3–11; it is also reprinted in Ian Hamilton (ed.), *The Modern Poet: Essays from the Review*, Macdonald, London 1968, pp. 101–10.

suggestion that the streets are located in time as well as place reminds us of our own eventual visitation.

Threatening our humanity, and standing for so much of what we fear, the ambulance itself takes on menacing overtones. So quietly are the symbolic suggestions allowed to emerge from the poem that by the time we reach the final stanza 'traffic' means not only vehicles but all human dealings or intercourse.[10] The general feeling is of the known and familiar breaking up, and the relentlessness of this process is mirrored in the poem's relentless and cumulative rhythmic pressure; for, with the exception of the final line, only two of the last ten lines are end-stopped as the poem carries us to its destination. Furthermore, ends and beginnings become confused. In the penultimate stanza 'borne', meaning 'carried', also holds the sense of 'birth', the pun being flashed into our minds by the 'deadened' later in the same line; and then later in this same stanza the coherence of something 'nearly at an end' 'begins' to loosen. As the poem develops, such tension impresses on us the feeling that things are falling apart.

Against the mundane details of the second stanza Larkin sets the terrifying impression of someone being carried into an ambulance, and we glimpse fleetingly a 'wild white face . . . As it is carried in and stowed'. The face, dehumanized by the pronoun 'it' as well as by the verb 'stowed', stands out starkly against the ordinariness of life going on as usual. Such dehumanization ensures that the appeals to 'we' and 'us' permit us no comfort, refuge, or security. The poem's impersonal manner has been used to hammer home something we know to be inescapably true, and in forcing us to recognize and confront it has increased our conscious understanding of a very ordinary experience.

Another development of Larkin's use of symbols in *The Whitsun Weddings* is his use of advertising imagery. He exploits common features of the urban scene to provide his depiction of human illusion with further dimensions. Department stores and billboards are, like ambulances, part of the city landscape most of us accept unthinkingly; yet advertising displays are designed both to create and to foster illusions, and Larkin uses such things as an additional means to explore humanity's tendency to self-deception. It is quite possible to read these poems as satirical exposés of the deviousness of the advertising media. Their design suggests that this is very much a subsidiary concern, however, for their stress is less on commercial exploitation than it is on the human readiness to respond to the lure of unreal needs. Specifically sociological approaches are equally

[10] This figurative sense of the word is now rare: see *OED*, 'traffic', sb. 3.

limiting. In 'The Large Cool Store' (p. 30), for example, any suggestion that Larkin is writing of a particular class 'Who leave at dawn low terraced houses/Timed for factory, yard and site' is firmly negated by the 'our' of the final stanza. Larkin's impulse is to reveal the general principle that in everyone there sleeps a sense of life lived according to fantasy.

At the beginning of this poem department store shorthand is interspersed with straightforward description, and also with commentary. This commentary is at first concentrated in a few terse words, such as 'conjures' and 'timed', but it comes to the fore at the end of the poem:

> To suppose
> They share that world, to think their sort is
> Matched by something in it, shows
>
> How separate and unearthly love is,
> Or women are, or what they do,
> Or in our young unreal wishes
> Seem to be . . .

The progression of the qualifications makes clear that the main subject of the poem is the unreality of human desire. The contrast of day and night, of everyday reality and unreal fantasy, is matched both by a colour contrast and a contrast between the display stands in which nighties seem to come alive and 'flounce' and those in which weekday clothes are set out 'plainly'. While remaining recognizably realistic and familiar the poem recreates the illusory images of modern life and modern love on which it comments. On one level it is a poem about sexploitation, but its darker purpose is to point beyond the human capacity for unreal idealization to the human need for fantasy.

The girl on the poster in 'Sunny Prestatyn' (p. 35) is equally 'separate and unearthly'. The poet first describes this poster, which is the poem's central metaphor, and then tells us what happened to it: 'She was slapped up one day in March'.

> . . . and the space
> Between her legs held scrawls
> That set her fairly astride
> A tuberous cock and balls
>
> Autographed *Titch Thomas* . . .

This poem is about turning on illusions which are so blatant as to be intolerable. Titch Thomas's response to the poster's implicit promise of sexuality is to rape it. The single sentence epitaph, 'She was too good for this life', is both true and sad, for the violence of the human response expresses an enraged insistence that the image on the poster accords with no reality whatsoever. With the exception of this single line, however, the poet allows his description to function as its own commentary; and as natural impulse reacts angrily against the imposition of an illusion, the final image of a cancer poster is a gruesomely appropriate emblem of nature in revolt.

The poet has remained detached. The passionate response comes from Titch Thomas, and is described dispassionately. 'Essential Beauty' (p. 42), in contrast, is a more direct and passionate use of advertising imagery. This poem is aimed at 'our live imperfect eyes', and all is confusion as we are plunged into the beginning of the poem:

> In frames as large as rooms that face all ways
> And block the ends of streets with giant loaves,
> Screen graves with custard, cover slums with praise
> Of motor-oil and cuts of salmon, shine
> Perpetually these sharply-pictured groves
> Of how life should be.

Not only is the main verb of this opening sentence held back until the end of the fourth line, as Timms has observed;[11] the clause governing this verb actually follows it, and thus our first task is to find our way around the inverted syntax. We are also in a Brobdingnagian world where streets are blocked off with loaves, a world of which the inverted values 'cover slums with praise' (the line-ending beautifully suggests that this clause is self-contained, so that the next line pours motor-oil and further confusion onto an already confusing scene), and a world in which salmon and motor-oil, graves and custard, are distastefully associated. The syntax of the sentence and the world it describes are equally mysterious, and we explore them simultaneously.

The formal shape of the poem destroys the mock-pastoral imagery it employs. The poem is divided into two sixteen-line verse paragraphs. Indeed, their identical structure permits us to call them stanzas. The first stanza establishes the illusory quality of huge billboard advertisements which the second one destroys by superimposing a vision of reality. Because the rhyme-scheme of the second half of the poem exactly repeats that of the first half, the layout of the poem is organized as visually as its

[11] Timms, *Philip Larkin*, p. 113.

imagery; and thus the effect of reading the second half of the poem is similar to that of superimposing one photographic negative on to another of the same scene. The second stanza removes the rose-coloured glasses. Nor do the visual correspondences between the two halves of the poem end with the rhyme-scheme. Only about a quarter of the lines are end-stopped, including the second, seventh, and fifteenth of each stanza; and as at the beginning of the twelfth line of the first stanza we learn that each hand 'stretches towards' the small cube for which it yearns, so at the beginning of the corresponding line in the second stanza such yearning is rewarded by a reciprocating image, to which attention is drawn by the repeated 'towards':

> . . . dying smokers sense
> Walking towards them through some dappled park
> As if on water that unfocused she
> No match lit up, nor drag ever brought near,
> Who now stands newly clear,
> Smiling, and recognising, and going dark.

Death intrudes dramatically, exposing the cruelty of an illusion which had promised salvation.

This falsely apocalyptic ending is far more than a comment on the use of sex to sell tobacco. By means of an appeal to our shared experience of what we see around us in the city, Larkin probes the visual images of advertising, not to tell us that smoking may be a health hazard, but to show us that we should not be taken in by the illusions to which the human mind is always prone where the things it yearns for are concerned. Working as it does in terms of advertising imagery, therefore, this poem's appeal is almost entirely visual. Furthermore the pattern of its concerns is enacted before us on the page by the devices governing the shape of the poem, which thus mimetically dismantles the illusions against which it is directed. We are given less explicit directions than in either 'The Large Cool Store' or 'Sunny Prestatyn', but the impact of this poem is more powerful and dramatic because of its careful control. The poet's attitudes, completely submerged in the technique, transform what advertising offers as universal symbols of happiness. The poet has diffused himself into aspects of the formal shape of the poem, thereby manipulating us into a perspective from which we can perceive the total meaning offered by the poem. A dramatic speaker has been replaced by an equally dramatic technical format.

If the advertising poems interpret the urban scene for us, then 'Here'

(p. 9) gives us a comprehensive overview of the world of *The Whitsun Weddings*. It literally sets the scene for most of the poems in the book, as its movement sweeps us over changing visual impressions. The first stanza 'Gathers to the surprise of a large town', where

> . . . residents from raw estates, brought down
> The dead straight miles by stealing flat-faced trolleys,
> Push through plate-glass swing doors to their desires— . . .

This landscape, obviously dotted with posters and large cool stores, is the home of Arnold and Mr Bleaney. The sweep of the first long sentence, the impetus it gets from the thrice-used 'swerving' in the first stanza, carries us through to the last stanza, to the thrice-used 'Here' at the beginning of the short sentences in the last few lines. The overall movement, which is from darkness to light, from shadows to the sun, whisks us across both landscape and townscape, and incorporates also 'A cut-price crowd, urban yet simple, dwelling/Where only salesmen and relations come'. The essence of this panoramic view is loneliness—the last stanza begins and the first sentence ends by clarifying this word—although the world we see is neither judged harshly nor presented in futile terms. John Wain's comparison of Larkin with L. S. Lowry is surely relevant here,[12] for the poet's vision is far from negative: we can see his fulsome response emerging through such adjectives as 'rich', 'gold', and 'shining'. Finally the poem takes us beyond the urban to the natural world which, although not beautiful in any conventional sense, represents freedom of a kind:

> Here silence stands
> Like heat. Here leaves unnoticed thicken,
> Hidden weeds flower, neglected waters quicken,
> Luminously-peopled air ascends . . .

The 'Luminously-peopled air' keeps us aware of humanity in a world which, as the words 'unnoticed', 'hidden', and 'neglected' suggest, survives independent of human activity. The things we see growing and coming to life here in the poem are no more beautiful than the urban 'pastoral' we saw earlier, but the vision is inclusive: the natural incorporates both the urban and the human, and all are integrated by the poem's directing overview. The world of the poem, and indeed of the book, is here literally compressed into the many hyphenated compounds of the second and third stanzas, and framed by the natural world of the

---

[12] Wain, 'Engagement or Withdrawal?', p. 173.

first and fourth stanzas. Without moving to a statement, this poem simply puts the world of the book before us to look at as we enter it.

The poet does not comment. His own distance is neutral. He remains detached from the scene, and we share his detachment. The first poem in *The Less Deceived* shows us a speaker looking over a photograph album, and Larkin manipulates the reader in such a way as to create an analogy between the speaker's relationship to the album and the reader's relationship to the poem. The visual manipulation of the first poem in *The Whitsun Weddings* is cinematic: instead of the 'swivel eye' of the earlier poem we have a moving camera, the technique being similar to that of a film director who organizes our perceptions of what he wants to show us. (It is worth recalling at this point that both 'At Grass' and 'Faith Healing' were inspired by films.) At his least tangible, Larkin is at his most manipulative; for we accept, with him, the world he shows us.

Whereas 'Here' shows us contemporary England, 'MCMXIV' (p. 28) directs our eyes to the England of the past. Once again we are *shown* the poet's impressions in such a way as to allow us to share them; but in contrast to 'Here', where we are quickly and constantly moving across the scenery of the poem, in 'MCMXIV' ('1914' lacks the 'monumental' impact of the roman numerals) we could be lingering over a photograph album and looking at images of pre-first war innocence. The four stanzas comprise a single sentence which, lacking a main verb, freezes the picture into complete stasis, and our eyes move across it with the poet's. The result is that a detailed and evocative picture is presented to the mind's eye, whether Larkin is describing a photograph or not. From the faces, advertisements, and children playing, we move out into the countryside: the visual details take us away from specific locations—the 'place-names all hazed over'—into a timeless past, 'Shadowing Domesday lines/Under wheat's restless silence'. This static, silent world is about to be blown apart:

> Never such innocence,
> Never before or since,
> As changed itself to past
> Without a word . . .
> Never such innocence again.

Our shared knowledge of subsequent events establishes a bond between poet and reader which both casts an elegiac aura over the whole poem and makes it very hard for us to disagree with his valuation of this lost world. Because the poem's attitudes are visualized rather than stated, the very gentleness of this poem's manner coerces us into accepting these attitudes along with the vantage-point we are given. As well as expressing Larkin's feeling for the England of the past, therefore, 'MCMXIV' also exemplifies Larkin's manipulative power. This poem tries to persuade, however gently.

I wish to conclude this discussion by looking briefly at two poems which leave behind loss, boredom, fear, dread, and isolation, and which celebrate human love. The differences in manner between the title poem and 'An Arundel Tomb' also define and encompass the technical diversity of this collection, for whereas 'An Arundel Tomb' relies on a central visual image and a muted authorial presence, a dramatic speaker and a multitude of sights and sounds are crucial to 'The Whitsun Weddings' (p. 21). The speaker here is the integrating force of the poem. Larkin has said, of writing this poem that 'the work all had to go into recreating the whole experience which came all at once and which as it built up slowly through the afternoon I knew could be a poem'.[13] As a dramatic projection of the poet, therefore, the speaker is the means by which the power of the experience is condensed and presented, although his individuality is far less important than the representativeness of the weddings he describes. His account of what he saw and thought on his train journey to London gradually builds up a powerful sense of the significance of marital union, and we are reminded by 'a religious wounding' that these marriages are celebrated in the context of a religious festival. (Whitsunday is the seventh Sunday after Easter, and commemorates the descent of the Holy Spirit upon the Apostles on the Day of Pentecost. The poet's journey is on the Saturday.)

The poem begins in solitude, and the reader shares the speaker's remembered perception of his journey. The particularity of the details keeps us alive to what the speaker sees and smells, and the main subject grows out of these sense-impressions:

> At first, I didn't notice what a noise
>   The weddings made
> Each station that we stopped at: sun destroys
> The interest of what's happening in the shade,
> And down the long cool platform whoops and skirls
> I took for porters larking with the mails,
> And went on reading.

As the weddings force themselves into the speaker's mind he becomes

[13] Larkin says this on the recording of *The Whitsun Weddings*.

obsessed with them, and his vantage-point affords him a perspective of balanced detachment which the reader shares. We observe the junctures and moments of transition in the lives of others; and there is a rich tension in the poem between something ending and something else beginning, which reaches a climax at the end of the poem as the tightening brakes inspire an image of release. What the speaker sees is complemented by what he cannot see. He gathers what is happening largely from the expressions of those he sees on the platform, until 'loaded with the sum of all they saw,/We hurried towards London'. The shift from 'they' to 'we' poises the speaker perfectly between detachment and involvement. Without being able to see the married couples who have joined the train, he is nevertheless conscious of sharing their journey. When they are all aboard he finds himself looking at the landscape and imagining the couples looking at it as well:

> A dozen marriages got under way.
> They watched the landscape, sitting side by side
> —An Odeon went past, a cooling tower,
> And someone running up to bowl—and none
> Thought of the others they would never meet
> Or how their lives would all contain this hour.
> I thought of London spread out in the sun,
> Its postal districts packed like squares of wheat . . .

As the train goes from north to south the poem unfolds itself against a representative English landscape, and all is deliberately depersonalized. Thus 'they', in the second line quoted above, refers to the 'marriages' of the previous line rather than to individuals, and again we must remember that the speaker has not seen his travelling companions. He is the unifying consciousness of the poem, and he insists that this consciousness is his alone: the contrast between 'none thought' and 'I thought' stresses both his detachment and his capacity to draw out the essential importance and value of what he has observed and imagined.

There is nothing condescending about this. Beneath smutty jokes and jewellery substitutes lies an event of genuine communal significance. 'They' and 'I' blend in the insistent 'we' of the final stanza, and the speaker's imaginative response takes over as the poem concludes:

> . . . We slowed again,
> And as the tightened brakes took hold, there swelled
> A sense of falling, like an arrow-shower
> Sent out of sight, somewhere becoming rain.

Only the 'coincidence' is 'frail'. The promise and power it holds are not. The meditation initially grew out of the speaker's sensations, and now his physical sense of the brakes' tension suggests to him metaphors of released power and transformation. At the very end of the poem his feelings are translated into the figurative language of plenitude and fruition. And yet it is characteristic of Larkin that such language should contain its own qualification. There is, for example, a tension between the images of rain and wheat: rain hinders the harvest. As Calvin Bedient has said: 'here at the close, at the same time that it gives the energy of life and the fruition of time their due, even as arrows speed and rain promises germination, it also makes us aware of inevitable dissolution, as arrows fall and rain means mould, dampness, the cold, the elemental'.[14] The speaker's detachment enables him to add the qualification here, but the power is not denied, and the metaphors release the power from confinement in any localized time or place. An awareness of the eternal and the elemental (of which, after all, death is a part) has grown naturally out of casual description, and has been concentrated and distilled in the mind of the speaker.

The speaker in 'The Whitsun Weddings' is the focal-point of the action. We see everything through him; we are constantly observing him, and for us he is the poem. In contrast the poet does not project himself at all in 'An Arundel Tomb' (p. 45), and the action of this poem is the reader's participation in a meditation on a single visual image. Again, however, the meditation is dramatic:

> Side by side, their faces blurred,
> The earl and countess lie in stone,
> Their proper habits vaguely shown
> As jointed armour, stiffened pleat,
> And that faint hint of the absurd—
> The little dogs under their feet.

Our eyes have not yet focused properly. Everything is unclear: 'blurred', 'vaguely', 'faint', the possible pun in 'lie'. The effigy is kept constantly before us, and the development of the poem is a gradual clarification of its meaning:

> Such plainness of the pre-baroque
> Hardly involves the eye, until

[14] Calvin Bedient, *Eight Contemporary Poets*, Oxford University Press, London 1974, p. 93.

> It meets his left-hand gauntlet, still
> Clasped empty in the other; and
> One sees, with a sharp tender shock,
> His hand withdrawn, holding her hand.

The experience is generalized into 'the eye' and 'one sees', but our eyes are directed to the significant visual detail which is brought into close-up. Thus the whole poem is brought to bear on an apparently minor detail. After evoking the passing centuries (and the poem remains strikingly visual) it returns us to the tomb, and as it does so the 'our' and 'us' of the final stanza shock us into realizing that Larkin has had the reader as firmly by the hand as the earl has had the countess. The destination of the mutual journey of poet and reader is the reinterpretation of the image:

> Time has transfigured them into
> Untruth. The stone fidelity
> They hardly meant has come to be
> Their final blazon, and to prove
> Our almost-instinct almost true:
> What will survive of us is love.

Paradoxically the tomb has brought to life an attitude. The stone symbolizes the survival of love, which it never was intended to do. However, the ironic and punning relationship of 'stone fidelity' and 'hardly' ensures that the poem ends with a rigorous and subtle series of qualifications, for this poet never allows us to entertain unreal expectations. Thus we are prevented from allowing the future tense of the last line to look too far ahead by the repeated 'almost' in the previous line. And the poem's final rhyme finely offers itself as an image of the effigy's significance: the last word of the poem, 'love', is both 'proved' and qualified by the word with which it does not share a full rhyme. The poem, and indeed the book, thus ends on a note of careful qualification and balance. Our eyes are fixed on the final word as closely as they have been watching the effigy for most of the poem, but our full assent is withheld by our memory and our sight of the almost-rhyming 'prove'. Lying on the page, the conceptual relationship of these words is as true as their rhyming one: it is 'almost true'. Our attention has been shifted from the effigy to its suggestive meaning which, with all its inbuilt tension, is realized as well as stated.

The Whitsun Weddings takes up and extends many features of *The Less Deceived*, although it contains fewer poems in the elusive manner of 'Dry-Point'. Indeed many of the poems make their points with such admirable directness that they render comment ponderous as well as superfluous. About 'Nothing To Be Said' (p. 11), for example, there is very little to be said. The continuity between these collections is technical as well as thematic. In each of them, a mask or speaker is frequently used. Their imagery appeals to the visual sense, and their stylistic devices appeal to the eye as well as to the ear. In addition, since *The North Ship* Larkin has used rhyme both efficiently and sensitively.[15] Yet *The Whitsun Weddings* is more interesting and valuable for its new departures. The images of the past and the illusions of the future that pervade the metaphorical world of *The Less Deceived* here gain tangibility from their local habitation in an urban landscape, the landscape to which we are welcomed in the first poem. The poems preserve an air of familiarity however symbolic they may be, and thus they have the effect of probing beneath the surface of everyday reality. Our recognition of the subjects he writes about renders the depths of the poet's perceptions accessible to us. Furthermore, Larkin's ever-present awareness of life's disappointments is not permitted, in this book, to turn in on itself, and the poetic treatment of selfhood and identity is characterized by a growing sophistication in the use of distancing devices.

Because it ranges more widely over human life, this book is also more comprehensive than *The Less Deceived*. It offers more of life's possibilities more convincingly, and the longest poem (which also gives the book its title) is a poem of celebration although its manner is detached. Others have the experience, the poet gives it meaning. Occasionally the visual technique becomes cinematic, when the poet transmutes his own presence into a manipulation of our view of the scene before us in the poem. This manner is impersonal and objective, yet the poet is never too distant because we always feel that he is sharing the experience with us. Larkin is as manipulative as Pope. When he is at his most detached his strategy is to *persuade* his reader into accepting a poem's moral point of view. So lightly does he insist on his own presence, however, that the effect created is less that of the poet projecting himself than of the reader gradually being drawn into the gravitational pull of the poems' concerns. And poems which do rely on authoritative commentary, such as 'Faith Healing', are effective because of their capacity to offer generalizations that we perceive to be authentic: in everyone there surely does sleep a sense of life lived according to love. That may even be a truism, but this poem has earned its right to generalize by its illumination of our thinking about human love.

[15] Larkin: 'I think one has to be both sensitive and efficient', Ian Hamilton interview, p. 249.

Not all the poems aspire to such authority, however, and the scope of the poems discussed in this chapter suggests the profusion of *The Whitsun Weddings*. The poems show us, by various means and from varying perspectives, our common urban environment, and our common patterns of thought and behaviour, in a new light or from an unusual point of view. This fine marriage of the familiar with the unexpected makes *The Whitsun Weddings* Larkin's most satisfying collection of poems.

IV

High Windows

Two years before the publication of *High Windows* Larkin said: 'There is great pressure on writers to "develop" these days: I think the idea began with Yeats, and personally I'm rather sceptical of it. What I should like to do is write different kinds of poems that might be by different people. Someone once said that the great thing is not to be different from other people, but different from yourself'.[1] This comment conveniently introduces *High Windows*, in which many poems are quite different from anything previously written by Larkin. Whether we regard this as development or fragmentation, it is certain that the cohesive energy of *The Whitsun Weddings* has broken out in new directions. There are, to be sure, substantial links and similarities with Larkin's earlier work, but as well as building on old structures the poet is also laying stones in uncharted territory. The results are fascinating.

The opening poem 'To the Sea' (p. 9) plunges us into an obsessive concern with ritual and continuity, human ritual and natural continuity, which is central to many poems in this book:

> To step over the low wall that divides
> Road from concrete walk above the shore
> Brings sharply back something known long before—
> The miniature gaiety of seasides.

Larkin believes that every poem 'is an action of some sort',[2] and here the opening infinitive compels the reader to share it. Stepping over the low wall is as much a psychological act, a conscious effort to conjure up the past, as it is a physical action, and it immediately engages the reader. By

---

[1] Radio broadcast to mark Larkin's fiftieth birthday, *The Listener*, 88 (July–December 1972), p. 209.
[2] Interview with Raymond Gardner, *The Guardian*, 31 March 1973, p. 12.

telling us what he sees at the same time as he explains its significance, the poet constantly fuses memories with visual impressions of the scene before him, and his surprise that 'all of it' is 'still going on' suggests something in which he participated long ago yet which has remained unchanged in his absence. He does remain distanced, however: 'miniature gaiety' implies perspective. His complex relationship to the scene has been established by his childhood, and indeed by his parentage:

> . . . happy at being on my own,
> I searched the sand for Famous Cricketers,
> Or, farther back, my parents, listeners
> To the same seaside quack, first became known.

Part of the scene in the past, he is 'strange to it' now. His balanced perspective as participant in the past and observer in the present gives him a vantage-point from which to draw out the meaning and significance of the scene as 'half an annual pleasure, half a rite'; for as the detail is organized by the meditative vision of the observer, the idea of ritual comes to the fore. Thus the title of this poem is a dedication to the sea as well as a pointer to the subject of going to the seaside.

As the scene changes and the families disappear before the observer's eyes, so also do his memories. This dramatic change in perspective prepares for the final comments; the 'cloudless scene' becomes clouded over 'like breathed-on glass', and the speaker reflects that the limitations of the individual life, our own inevitable 'falling short' of flawless weather, are offset by the natural pattern of unconscious growth and continuity between generations. The annual pilgrimage to the sea—'Coming to water' suggests ritual worship—is at once half-comic, slightly ludicrous, and intuitive. The act is indeed quite un*self*conscious, as the punning of 'habit' and 'undressed' reminds us, and also instinct with a significance of which the participants are largely unaware.

The central idea of continuity is underscored by the rhyming patterns of the poem. The penultimate line of each stanza has no rhyming counterpart within its own stanza, but it anticipates the second and third lines of the following stanza, and thus is echoed by them. At the end of the final stanza the pattern is rounded off by an authoritative couplet which brings the generations together, but the pattern ensures that none of the stanzas is self-contained by either rhyme or syntax. Moreover the participles of the final sentence—'falling', 'coming', 'teaching', 'clowning'—reinforce continuity by leaving us with the impression of something continuously going on.

A poem which on the surface describes provincial English behaviour also suggests religious observance, pagan ritual, even fertility rite. J. R. Watson has pointed out that the language of this poem is 'suggestive of ritual', and Alan Brownjohn, reviewing *High Windows*, has drawn attention to 'the greatly strengthened fascination with the value of habits and rituals'[3] in the poems generally. 'Show Saturday' (p. 37) is the most explicit expression of that value. The descriptive profusion of the first five stanzas ranges across multiple impressions as it recreates the sights and sounds of the show in the poem's assonance, alliteration, and bustling syntax. Phrases and clauses are thrown together, like the impressions they reflect, with the barest minimum of connective emphasis. The reader's eye is guided from detail to detail, and everything is held together by the overlapping rhymes unifying each long stanza. Finally the meaning is directly stated, and the poem moves through generalization to benediction:

> Let it stay hidden there like strength, below
> Sale-bills and swindling; something people do,
> Not noticing how time's rolling smithy-smoke
> Shadows much greater gestures; something they share
> That breaks ancestrally each year into
> Regenerate union. Let it always be there.

The three gradually shortening final sentences, spread over twenty-two lines, crystallize both the meaning of the poem and the significance of the show. The poem is almost totally without metaphor, thus remaining at the level of naturalistic description until this explanation is offered. The show's significance as a ritualistic public gesture is unperceived by the participants, although the mass of humanity described in the poem represents an unconscious community of feeling. For the people involved the show is just 'something' they 'do' and 'share', but it enables them to transcend their private lives while never ceasing to be themselves. In that lies its contribution to the human sense of community. Like going to the seaside, the show is repeated, seasonal, and shared, and it likewise represents community and continuity.

In these poems Larkin's feeling for common human behaviour is established in a social context. His familiar method of symbol and commentary is here extended to include social behaviour (it is worth

---

[3] J. R. Watson, 'The Other Larkin', *Critical Quarterly*, 17 (1975), p. 356; Alan Brownjohn, 'The Deep Blue Air', *New Statesman*, 87 (January–June 1974), p. 854.

pointing out that the urban landscapes of *The Whitsun Weddings* are often without people). These poems celebrate meaningful human gestures, associating them with various times of the year to give them a place in the seasonal calendar. In stark opposition, 'Forget What Did' (p. 16) begins by evoking discontinuity:

> Stopping the diary
> Was a stun to memory,
> Was a blank starting . . .

The stop-start movement of the verse—this stanza begins with 'stopping' and ends with 'starting'—dramatizes discontinuity, and the poem goes on to express dissatisfaction with the limited perspectives afforded by human time and individual memory. The poem places things both remembered and not remembered against things recurrent but unnoticed. A desire is expressed to see the self as part of the cyclical rhythms of nature rather than in terms of the trivial occurrences with which a diary might ordinarily be filled. Only by setting the events of our lives against the 'celestial recurrences' of the seasonal cycle can we see them in the context of natural continuity.

However, it is enormously difficult to put human life in such a perspective. Nature's unconsciously repeated rituals bring intimations of mortality as well as of continuity, and many of the best poems in *High Windows* express this tension:

> The trees are coming into leaf
> Like something almost being said;
> The recent buds relax and spread,
> Their greenness is a kind of grief.
>
> Is it that they are born again
> And we grow old? No they die too.
> Their yearly trick of looking new
> Is written down in rings of grain.
>
> Yet still the unresting castles thresh
> In fullgrown thickness every May.
> Last year is dead, they seem to say,
> Begin afresh, afresh, afresh.
>
> ('The Trees', p. 12)

The cyclical pattern of the stanza (abba) enacts nature's cycles, and the participles generate the idea of movement. Repetition and renewal coincide in the final line of the poem, but the sounds of the poem have also reinforced the sense of repetition within change by means of echo within certain lines: 'greenness'/'grief', 'written'/'rings', 'still'/'unresting'. The total effect of the poem belies its apparent simplicity: it creates a mysterious sense of correspondence between human and natural that is too elusive for direct statement. Something is *almost* being said.

Much, however, is hinted at, such as an analogy between human life and the life of trees. That mortality is a condition of creative vitality is suggested in the second stanza, for nature writes poems too: 'Their yearly trick of looking new/Is written down in rings of grain'. The creative correspondence between man and nature is further promoted by the stanza form, which imitates the rings on a tree trunk. The puns on 'grain' and 'thresh' similarly nudge growth and fulfilment into life, as does the abundant thickness of fullgrown trees. The poem stops just short of imparting consciousness to nature.

The total effect of all this is that the poem itself stops just short of explicitly saying much about the similarities between natural and human life. Moreover, there are ways in which the poem's shape and manner contrive to work against its statements. The poem asks whether the essential difference between man and nature is that man is not reborn, and then answers this question by saying, of the trees, 'No, they die too'. But the final stanza takes us back to the trees' renewal: even if they only 'seem to say' that 'last year is dead', their message is still 'begin afresh'. There is a rich tension in the poem between the poet's certain knowledge that *all* life is slow dying and his wonder at the new-found vitality of nature every spring. In spite of its assertions that trees die the poem ends with images of their rebirth, but on the other hand the poet's wonder is qualified by his awareness of human mortality. And because the poem's perceptions of inanimate nature are shaded by a consciousness of mortal humanity, the poem is primarily an elegy for man. In 'Cut Grass' (p. 41), too, the natural world is used for what it can suggest about the human world, and again the poet is ambivalent about the lessons nature holds for man:

> Cut grass lies frail:
> Brief is the breath
> Mown stalks exhale . . .

The vital smell of new-mown grass is a reminder of its (and our) mortality, just as the brevity of the poem's lines imitates the precarious balance of life. In addition, the second line equates 'brevity' with 'breath', which in turn rhymes with 'death'; and because of its association with snow the repeated 'white' forces the idea of winter upon us in the midst of summer. Death is rarely far beneath the surface in any poem by Larkin, and his response to natural beauty is suffused with his awareness of human mortality. We should not be surprised that this is so, given the nature of this poet's interests, but as Larkin's first concentrated use of inanimate nature these poems do represent something of a new departure.

It is characteristic of Larkin that these poems permit no idealization of nature. The tendency of art to idealize generally is viciously debunked in 'The Card-Players' (p. 23), another poem as utterly unlike anything Larkin wrote before *High Windows* as it is unlike anything else in the book.

The poem comments on the relationship between art and reality, but its standpoint is confusing in that it both proclaims and makes fun of the idea of elemental unity between man and nature.[4] Perhaps it would be truer to say that the poem takes a light-hearted look at the particular kind of painting it recreates for us. It is possible that the title alludes to a lost work by Brueghel, which depicted quarrelling card-players;[5] and if this is the case it explains the Dutch names and also gives us a clearer idea of the nature of the painting recreated: the drinking and scatalogical references would be typical of Brueghel, whose paintings are characterized by an earthy awareness of the community of man and nature. Larkin takes the reader-spectator from detail to detail in the painting, and is careful to evoke the sense most elusive to the visual artist, the sense of sound. However, he does this in such a way as to reduce the human to its animal aspects, for the sounds are of people croaking, belching, snoring, and farting.

With deliberate earthiness, therefore, the poem insists on the relationship of human and natural. They are linked by the elements of earth, air, fire, and water: Jan 'pisses' into the rain and mud, Dirk lights his pipe from the fire, Prijck 'snores with the gale'. Their names are no loftier than their activities: in this poem everything is reduced to the physical. The poem's fourth inhabitant is glimpsed croaking 'scraps of songs . . . about love' while he eats, the word *scraps* effectively equating

---

[4] Roger Day, to whose account of the poem my own is generally indebted, suggests that 'Larkin is making a point about the relationship between art and reality': see *Philip Larkin*, The Open University Press, Milton Keynes 1976, p. 34.
[5] This painting is mentioned by Svetlana and Paul Alpers, '*Ut Pictura Noesis?* Criticism in Literary Studies and Art History' in R. Cohen (ed.), *New Directions in Literary History*, Routledge and Kegan Paul, London 1974, p. 206.

the songs with his meal. Lest we are still in any danger of idealizing anything, especially love, Jan's final, accidental bull's-eye should wake us to our senses, or at least remind us of them, as he 'farts,/Gobs at the grate, and hits the queen of hearts'. This is indeed 'bestial', and it is also to some extent 'secret'; for although their activities place Jan, Dirk and Prijck in unity with nature, they remain separate activities. When we see them they are all totally self-involved, and not playing cards at all.[6] The point may be that the most elemental forms of human activity are those of which we are least conscious, and which show us to least advantage, but this may be taking the poem too seriously by failing to account for its mocking, debunking tone. In any case, the whole thrust of the poem is negative: it works *against* idealization.

Although we may feel tempted to describe this poem as a lesson or exercise in artistic method, its archness remains evasive. In recreating an imaginary painting Larkin puts his capacities for the realization of visual effects to a new use, yet the reader is manipulated to little effect. If the poem does invoke Brueghel, it cheats by excluding both his humanity and his moral perspective; and, in spite of Larkin's cleverness, the poem achieves very little. In 'The Trees', on the other hand, the poet allowed his perplexity to emerge naturally from the description, and that poem's apparent slightness supports great emotional weight. 'The Card-Players' lacks both such solidity, and also the human vision of 'To the Sea'. It remains an unfortunately 'artistic' poem.

Another new feature of *High Windows* is the inclusion of poems dealing with topical subjects. Whether we call them political poems, or 'condition-of-England' poems, they are less than satisfactory. 'Going, Going' (p. 21) was commissioned by the Department of the Environment, and its weaknesses are attributable to its being a commissioned poem. Its lack of a clear focus betrays the lack of a firm governing idea, for what is offered as a poem about the environment turns out to be a poem about growing old:

> Chuck filth in the sea, if you must:
> The tides will be clean beyond.
> —But what do I feel now? Doubt?
>
> Or age, simply? The crowd

---

[6] Such self-involvement is a feature of some of Brueghel's best-known paintings. A close look at 'The Blue Cloak', for example, reveals many people engaged in utterly discrete activities, the overall unity of which is apparent only to the perceiver.

Is young in the M1 café;
Their kids are screaming for more—
More houses, more parking allowed,
More caravan sites, more pay.

The poem is more about the conservative Englishman's fear of philistine commercialism than about pollution, and it is infected by the crudity it so strongly deplores. Pleasant things are opposed to unpleasant people: on one hand we have shadows, meadows, guildhalls and carved choirs, and on the other we have louts, crooks, and tarts. The contempt here is distasteful; and the slangy colloquialisms—'snuff it', and 'the whole boiling'—suggest the poet's unease about his poem. Lack of subtlety complements lack of direction. Commercial exploitation and a feeling of personal loss are yoked by violence together, and the poem falls flatly on its lame final line: 'I just think it will happen, soon'. Although the concept of continuity is extended into the public sphere it is never free from the personal sense of growing old. 'Homage to a Government' (p. 29), which has a more tangible political direction, also expresses the need for continuity in public, national life:

Next year we shall be living in a country
That brought its soldiers home for lack of money . . .
Our children will not know it's a different country.
All we can hope to leave them now is money.

The aggressive dating of the poem (1969) limits the question of England's heritage to an attack on the then Labour Government's defence policy. It would be hard both to disagree with Larkin's political bias and to admire the poem, but there are technical difficulties as well. The deadpan irony associated with the phrase 'it is all right' is too defensive for such a poem—its effect is to turn the aggression away from its target—and the redundant non-rhymes render the poem simply rather than ironically complacent.[7] It refuses to argue. The point made in the second stanza about the randomness of so much of human experience is a familiar one in Larkin's poetry, but here it is not consistent with the palpable design of a highly polemical poem.

Neither of these poems does anything like justice to the strength of Larkin's feeling for tradition and continuity in English life. Neither poem

[7] John Wain disagrees. He argues that the form contributes to the poem's satirizing of 'self-enclosed pettiness' and 'lack of imagination': see 'The Poetry of Philip Larkin', *Malahat Review*, 39 (1976), p. 103.

faces up to the social or political issues it raises, and both reduce Larkin's feelings to a series of crude socio-political assumptions. The impoverishment of these poems is revealed by comparison with 'MCMXIV' from *The Whitsun Weddings*, which can justly be described as a pre-political poem, which evokes rather than states, and which lingers on the positive qualities of the past rather than on the dreadfulness of the present. By directing us to what has been lost, the muted manner of 'MCMXIV' unobtrusively musters Larkin's poetic strengths, whereas these poems reveal only weaknesses. Strong convictions do not of themselves make for strong poems.

Such crudity is rare in Larkin's poetry, and especially in the poems in this book, which generally treat familiar subjects with increased sophistication. The related subjects of identity and loneliness are given wider dimensions than previously, and are approached from fresh angles. 'The Old Fools' (p. 19) makes its points in relation to age generally:

> At death, you break up: the bits that were you
> Start speeding away from each other for ever
> With no one to see.

Death is the fragmentation of the self as well as extinction, terrifying because we can only see such fragmentation in the deaths of others. At the end of the poem we are chillingly reminded that old age may come as a 'hideous inverted childhood' to all who live long enough, but the poem makes clear that the dislocation old people experience between past and present is constantly with us in human life, always ready to disrupt our sense of life's continuity:

> That is where they live:
> Not here and now, but where all happened once.
> This is why they give
>
> An air of baffled absence, trying to be there
> Yet being here.

The poem's treatment of age and death reflects upon all of human life, and leaves us with the impression of the self as a series of spots of time that get harder to integrate as life develops.

Self-consciousness is held at arm's length. 'Posterity' (p. 27) opens dramatically: 'Jake Balokowsky, my biographer,/Has this page microfilmed'. *This* page? The device simply but forcibly thrusts the disjunction between image and reality before our eyes; and the poem then continues as a blistering attack on the self-centred academic, who is clearly frustrated with his biographical subject: 'I'm stuck with this old fart at least a year'. As well as looking satirically at the American academic, however, the poet is also having a self-deprecating glance at himself from the point of view of his imaginary biographer. There is more than a hint of the poet's self-consciousness in Balokowsky's final description of his subject as 'One of those old-type *natural* fouled-up guys'; and the poem thus ends with our attention equally divided between poet and biographer. Balokowsky's inhumanity and the poet's ordinariness offset each other, and the humour further distances the self-conscious aspects of the poem; for Balokowsky is totally *un*selfconscious, and by allowing the poet to look outward as well as at himself the satirical thrust against his imaginary biographer works as a mask for the poet, and therefore is a self-distancing device. We observe them both.

Both poet and reader are distanced, in 'Friday Night in the Royal Station Hotel' (p. 18), as detached observers of an impressive visualization of loneliness. Isolation, exile, loneliness, are all terms used by the poem, and they are supported by what can only be called a concrete absence of people. From the first words, all is visual and paradoxical: 'light spreads darkly'. Even silence is 'laid like carpet', the simile providing a physical correlative for the awareness of a quality of absence. Inanimate things govern verbs we normally associate with human activities, as the chairs 'face' each other and the dining-room 'declares'. Full ashtrays, shoeless corridors, empty chairs and beds are all before our eyes, and remain (as the title suggests) in the hotel until the final lines create larger perspectives: '*Now/Night comes on. Waves fold behind villages*'.[8] The poem expresses feelings of exclusion and exile by concentrating on the potent absence of others, and then by introducing the sense of a world elsewhere. At the end of the poem the Royal Station Hotel, which has filled the poem, suddenly becomes frighteningly small and insignificant.

Isolation, loneliness, and alienation, are characteristic features of Larkin's poetry, but in *High Windows* such things are treated more diversely than in his previous work. The progression from *The Less Deceived* through *The Whitsun Weddings* to *High Windows* is governed by an

---

[8] Kenneth Moon, 'Cosmic Perspective: A use of imagery in the Poetry of Philip Larkin', *Poetry Australia*, 68 (October 1978), pp. 59–63, draws attention to Larkin's persistent use of a 'distancing device' which 'consists of a raising of the poetic intensity, often sudden and brief, by resort to natural and frequently "cosmic" imagery—wind, clouds, sky, rain, night, sea, fields'. It 'seems always used to give this instant and illuminating reversal of perspective, a vastly more detached and long-sighted view of the poem's matter' (p. 59).

increasing willingness to present poems dramatically: this both enhances the variety of manner with which persistent concerns are presented, and also increases their accessibility to the experience of the reader. We may regard this as manipulation, persuasion, or even coercion, but its effect is to make the reader part of the drama by causing him to enact the poems' thoughts. Thus, while 'The Old Fools' does not use an 'I', the poet manipulates us dramatically by his use of pronouns, which unobtrusively draws us into the poem and which makes the poem's attitudes work upon us. For most of the poem the speaker uses 'they' and its forms to refer to 'the old fools', and 'you' and its forms when he wishes to generalize; but it is impossible not to feel that the second-person pronoun is not directed at us (or you) in some way. The poem therefore purports to give us something to contemplate while simultaneously encroaching on us, and the 'we' of the final stanza makes explicit the knowledge that has gradually been building up through the poem. (In fact the poem has begun subtly to involve us as early as the second stanza, which casually but strategically uses the same pronoun.) We may resent being made to share the attitudes which emerge from the poem, but the technique is indubitably effective. It locks the reader in the poem and leaves him with nowhere to go.

The poet's perspective has become the reader's, which makes the absence of an 'I' a crucial part of the strategy. There is not enough of a presence to react against, and hence we are made to feel and share dramatically the dislocation expressed in the poem. 'High Windows' (p. 17) is a further example of this strategy of involving the reader, and an excellent illustration of its effectiveness. Although this poem lacks the dramatic impetus of a particular situation, it is organized in such a way as to allow the reader to feel his kinship with the speaker. We are forced to *see* his meaning:

> When I see a couple of kids
> And guess he's fucking her and she's
> Taking pills or wearing a diaphragm,
> I know this is paradise . . .

The poem's perceptions are carried initially by the verbs 'see', 'guess', and 'know'. The subject of the poem is less the governing 'I' than it is the mental pattern established by these verbs.

Consciousness of self interacts with consciousness of others, and in the second stanza an image of discontinuity—'an outdated combine harvester'—is set against an image of continuity—'the long slide'. The speaker feels that there are choices open to others that were not available to him, but the feeling is universalized and externalized by the creation of a perspective shared by 'everyone old' on 'everyone young'. When the speaker begins considering his own youth he keeps himself clinically detached from it, for the consciousness he has now cannot possibly be attributed to himself as he was then. Another verb heralds the change in direction:

> I wonder if
> Anyone looked at me, forty years back,
> And thought, *That'll be the life*;
> *No God any more, or sweating in the dark*
>
> *About hell and that, or having to hide*
> *What you think of the priest. He*
> *And his lot will all go down the long slide*
> *Like free bloody birds.*

Suddenly, as he looks at his own youth from the point of view of someone else, the speaker has become two people in the poem. This fresh perspective establishes for him that his own feelings about youth's current freedom from sexual inhibitions are no different essentially from the way his elders used to imagine his freedom from religious inhibitions.

The poem changes direction yet again, and concludes in a manner reminiscent of 'Church Going' or 'The Whitsun Weddings'. The speaker fades into the background, and the poem focuses on its central image:

> And immediately
>
> Rather than words comes the thought of high windows:
> The sun-comprehending glass,
> And beyond it, the deep blue air, that shows
> Nothing, and is nowhere, and is endless.

The syntax here plays down the speaker's presence. The subject of the sentence is not himself; it is a 'thought' which 'comes' to resolve the imaginative tussle of the earlier verbs, and of course the absence of a pronoun here is essential to the poem's movement towards generalization.

The movement has been to detachment as well. The speaker's imagination is realized tangibly at first, but he gradually eliminates himself from the poem by diffusing his own identity into that of others: *everyone* old and *everyone* young. He presents himself in the poem as both representatively old and representatively young, and we blend ourselves with him not only because of this, but also because we share his visual perceptions and his final, visualized thought. At the poem's climax Larkin presides over the sympathetic fusion of reader and speaker, and the poem ends with reader, speaker, and poet all concentrating on the central image of the poem. Out of the speaker's dislocation has come aesthetic unity and force, and a poem that begins with exclusion ends in community.

Our awareness of the speaker conditions our response to this poem: the poem's perceptions are his perceptions. In *High Windows* Larkin exploits for extreme effect the device of a speaker or dramatic mask, and this aspect of his technique has undergone further refinements since *The Whitsun Weddings*. Sometimes, however, the manner is familiar. In 'Vers de Société' (p. 35) the speaker is mocking an invitation he has received:

> *My wife and I have asked a crowd of craps*
> *To come and waste their time and ours: perhaps*
> *You'd care to join us?* In a pig's arse, friend.
> Day comes to an end.
> The gas fire breathes, the trees are darkly swayed.
> And so *Dear Warlock-Williams: I'm afraid—* . . .

As the beginning of the conventional and polite expression of regret tails away into emptiness we realize that the fear is genuine, no matter how the sarcasm tries to cover it. The fear is equally evident in the clear, hostile impression the speaker receives when he looks out of the window 'to see the moon thinned/To an air-sharpened blade'. This poem is reminiscent of 'Dockery and Son', not only in its movement from a colloquial opening to a meditative conclusion but also in its deployment of rhyme. The pattern of the three rhymes in each stanza shifts as the poem develops, and the three couplets that we find in the opening stanza are not repeated until the final stanza. Technically, therefore, the poem comes full circle and finds the speaker where he was at the beginning; but the technical similarity between first and last stanzas invites us to think about the differences between the beginning and ending of the poem. The overall effect of this meditation on the meaning of social routines is to take the speaker from the contemptuous and flimsy 'certainties'[9] at the beginning of the poem to a wholly different kind of certainty at the end:

[9] Timms characterizes the speaker's initial manner well when he calls it 'impotent bravado': David Timms, *Philip Larkin*, Oliver and Boyd, Edinburgh 1973, p. 124.

Only the young can be alone freely.
The time is shorter now for company,
And sitting by a lamp more often brings
Not peace, but other things.
Beyond the light stand failure and remorse
Whispering *Dear Warlock-Williams: Why, of course—*

The acceptance of the invitation amounts to an acceptance of the fear of loneliness, the fear implicitly present from the beginning of the poem. The speaker has avoided all kinds of impending rationalizations, and in addition to his decision to go to the party he has moved outside himself in other ways; for as the poem develops he stops talking about himself and addresses himself to more general questions. He may not be able to answer them, but his cyclical journey broadens into a consideration of more than just himself. His admission at the end is not registered as a defeat because its honesty overrides the angry defences of the earlier part of the poem. Nor is it a conclusion: the rhyme-scheme comes full circle, and the poem ends without conclusive punctuation. 'Sad Steps' (p. 32) traces a similar path, in that the speaker again moves from thinking about himself, to the more generalized 'one', and then to 'others'. The speaker here is less defensive, caught unawares as he is:

Groping back to bed after a piss
I part thick curtains, and am startled by
The rapid clouds, the moon's cleanliness.

Four o'clock in the morning, and he feels excluded from his youth which looks back at him in the shape of the moon. The traditional symbolic associations of the moon—'Lozenge of love! Medallion of art!'—are deflated, and as the moon comes to stand in his mind for both his own youth and the youth of others he moves to a low-key conclusion:

The hardness and the brightness and the plain
Far-reaching singleness of that wide stare

Is a reminder of the strength and pain
Of being young; that it can't come again,
But is for others undiminished somewhere.

Parting the curtains at the beginning of the poem opens the way to a moral perception. The clarity of the language initially describing the scene is matched by later clarity of insight, and this movement is not obscured by the various tones of the speaking voice used in the poem. The mark of the poem's own clarity is its refusal to sentimentalize youth: by setting the strength of youth against its pain, and by ending with its emphasis on 'others', the poem comes to rest on a note of simultaneous resignation and consolation. It therefore recapitulates a saddening but inevitable realization which the speaker both exemplifies and expresses.

The speaker of 'This Be The Verse' (p. 30) also exemplifies the process he describes, but as a victim of it. Jaded and disillusioned as he is, he uses sardonic humour to mask the bitterness of his attitude to experience:

> They fuck you up, your mum and dad.
>   They may not mean to, but they do.
> They fill you with the faults they had
>   And add some extra, just for you.

The speaker tries to elevate his own perceptions to the level of general truths by translating them into proverbial or epigrammatic impersonality, but the nursery-rhyme lilt (as in 'Naturally the Foundation will Bear Your Expenses') is transparently revealing. His utterly negative conception of continuity fosters the impoverished advice: 'Get out as early as you can,/And don't have any kids yourself'. Humour masks bitterness, and the poem uses its speaker to take a swipe at the very fatalism of which Larkin has been accused. A different kind of humorous presence is used to make an equally serious point in 'Annus Mirabilis' (p. 34), which begins with the outrageous assertion that 'Sexual intercourse began/In nineteen sixty-three'.

> Sexual intercourse began
> In nineteen sixty-three
> (Which was rather late for me) —
> Between the end of the *Chatterley* ban
> And the Beatles' first LP.

The beautifully deadpan manner is a perfect surface from which an attitude to 'the permissive society' emerges. In each of these two poems the humour creates perspectives from which the reader has to make judgements both about what is said, and about the manner in which it is being said.

There is nothing strange about this to a reader familiar with Larkin's earlier poetry. Poems such as 'This Be The Verse' or 'Vers de Société' are no more acerbic than 'Send No Money' or 'Self's the Man', and most of the poems examined so far in this chapter do echo Larkin's previous work in various ways. 'Show Saturday' and 'Friday Night in the Royal Station Hotel' are variant exploitations of the cinematic outlook of 'Here' or the photographic focus of 'MCMXIV', and the authorial presence in 'To the Sea' recalls the detached observer of 'The Whitsun Weddings', both of these poems moving to generalizations. In 'The Old Fools' we are manipulated as cleverly as we are in 'Ambulances', and if 'High Windows' recalls 'Church Going' in the gradual replacement of the speaker with a more direct version of the poet it also recalls 'Talking in Bed' in that it enables us to share its generalized perceptions as they grow out of the poem's meditative movement. Sometimes, therefore, we are aware of a presence sharing things with us, at other times of a presence directing and showing us, at still other times of a presence intimidating us or making us laugh. The speaking voice works constantly as a mediator between poet and reader, and our awareness of it is crucial to Larkin's strategy.

It should also be clear by now, however, that much of *High Windows* represents a poetry of departures for Larkin. In 'The Card-Players' an aesthetic image is used to comment on the relationship of art and life; in 'Posterity' the double-edged thrust is directed both inwards and outwards; and 'The Trees' and 'Cut Grass' present us with natural symbols whose meaning is as elusive as it is suggestive. In many of the poems Larkin's stance is extremely hard to determine, and at times the poet disappears altogether, making it impossible to work out his relationship with the speaker of a poem. 'Sympathy in White Major' (p. 11), for example, can reasonably be termed an exercise in the poet's dextrous self-effacement. Indeed, the visual balance between the three stanzas established by the organization of the typography may suggest, like the punning title, that 'exercise' or 'composition' may be the most apt word to describe the poem. Initially the poem is very confusing. The pronouns 'I' and 'he' apparently refer to poet and major respectively, but as the poem progresses it seems that both pronouns refer to the major: his 'private pledge' is a pledge to himself. Therefore the 'sympathy' of the title involves the poet imagining himself 'in' the major, who in turn runs through the clichés by which others have praised him. This in turn engages our sympathy by taking us behind the blimpish façade. Nor do we doubt the sympathy of the poet, which has been attracted by a quality of misunderstood innocence. As the title originally suggested, therefore, the device of the poem, which involves the poet's assumption of the major's personality for the duration of the poem, is the substance of the poem.

It is virtually impossible to locate the poet in 'Livings' (p. 13), the longest and most disparate poem in *High Windows*. The three parts of this poem belong to three separate speakers: a small businessman, a lighthouse keeper, and an academic. Their reflections on their lives come from different historical points. We learn from the last line of the businessman's monologue that he is speaking in 1929, a fact which lends him pathos by hinting at impending disaster. The blanks of the first stanza are presumably intended to give him a representative status, but they additionally suggest that it matters little where he is. Having inherited a business from his father, he now finds himself trapped in it. The meaningless social ritual established by his father arouses an implicit consciousness of needs that his way of life does not answer, and the pointlessness of it all is stressed by the self-consciously punning reference to buying a round of drinks: 'I stand a round'/'I stand around'. In contrast, the academic speaker of the third part of the poem positively revels in the smallness of his world. He reduces all things, religious as well as political, to the level of gossip:

> The wine heats temper and complexion:
> Oath-enforced assertions fly
> On rheumy fevers, resurrection,
> Regicide and rabbit pie.

'Regicide' suggests that this is probably the seventeenth century, but the essential triviality of this way of life is the point.

The second section of this poem is the most fascinating. Short lines and Anglo-Saxon compounds dramatize an outburst of energy that is responsive to and in harmony with the world of nature:

> Seventy feet down
> The sea explodes upwards,
> Relapsing, to slaver
> Off landing-stage steps—
> Running suds, rejoice!

The reference to liners in the final stanza places the speaker in the twentieth century, but the time is less important than the location. Self-sufficient and secure, the speaker is isolated from the social world with which he obviously does not wish to be involved: 'Keep it all off!' His social communion extends no further than the sea and its creatures, to which he exclaims rapturously, "I cherish you!" His element is solitude, and his divining-cards endow him with authority as well as with mystery. Whether or not we agree with Alan Brownjohn's contention that the lighthouse suggests 'the poet's precarious vantage-point',[10] we surely feel that the poet's sympathies in 'Livings' lie with the god-like self-contained outsider whose relationships are to elemental things and whose life represents both solitude and communion with nature. The speakers of the three parts of this poem may be implicitly commenting on each other, but the objection remains that it leaves us with three poems under a single title. As a whole it is elusive; and elusiveness is rarely this poet's most successful mode.

It is for this reason that 'The Building' (p. 24) is the most powerful poem in *High Windows*. Although we do not know where we are being led, the manipulating presence of the poet is beside us from the moment (at the end of the second line) when we are first exhorted to 'see'. In many ways the technique is a familiar one: we have an image, and also a commentary on it, and as in 'At Grass' and 'An Arundel Tomb' the close involvement of the reader's visual sense ensures that we enact the drama of the poem for ourselves. Yet whereas in 'At Grass' we remain static observers of the distanced horses, and whereas in 'An Arundel Tomb' our eyes are focused on one detail, in this poem we are provided with multiple vantage-points from which to explore the symbolic building. The effective manipulation of our perspective on the various details marshalled before our eyes is to take us gradually inside the building. From beholding it at a distance we move through the entrance, through the waiting-room, until in the fifth stanza we suddenly realize that we are upstairs and looking outside. By the time Larkin chooses to tell us the meaning of his symbol we are firmly enclosed within it. An impassioned outcry heralds the first direct appeal to shared experience:

> —O world,
> Your loves, your chances, are beyond the stretch
> Of any hand from here! And so, unreal,
> A touching dream to which we all are lulled
> But wake from separately.

At this point (the seventh stanza) the poem begins its movement to direct statement.

The care taken over the construction of this poem is revealed by the

[10] Alan Brownjohn, *Philip Larkin*, Writers and their Work no. 247, Longmans, Harlow 1975, p. 19.

coexistence of a seven-line stanza with eight-line units of rhyme.[11] This division in the organization of the poem is functional and important. The structural movements of the thought tend to follow the pattern of the rhyme rather than of the stanza, the function of which is to carry us dramatically forward; for, with the sole exception of the first one, each stanza ends without punctuation of any kind. The effect of this is both to leave the reader struggling in vacancy for a split-second, and then to carry him further into the poem and the building. The construction of the poem is thus as artful as the construction of the building we are made to enter, and the Italian etymology of the word *stanza* (a room of a house) makes obvious this functional separation of stanza and rhyme-scheme.

The first two units of rhyme hint by simile and comparison at what the place is, but refuse actually to tell us. 'Higher than the handsomest hotel', it is nevertheless not a hotel. It is 'like an airport lounge' and 'like a local bus', although the things that draw up at the entrance are 'not taxis', and 'a kind of nurse' comes from time to time. Very early in the poem, however, the building is made to suggest the heart of life itself: 'All round it close-ribbed streets rise and fall/Like a great sigh out of the last century'. In reading the poem and in simultaneously finding our way around the building we are conscious of things going on, and even as we are being guided to the final statement we are conscious of a nurse parenthetically beckoning someone away. With the fifty-sixth line both a stanza and a unit of rhyme end, and the last eight lines—the final stanza and the detached final line—explicitly interpret the symbol for us. Of the people waiting

> All know they are going to die.
> Not yet, perhaps not here, but in the end,
> And somewhere like this. That is what it means,
> This clean-sliced cliff; a struggle to transcend
> The thought of dying, for unless its powers
> Outbuild cathedrals nothing contravenes
> The coming dark, though crowds each evening try
>
> With wasteful, weak, propitiatory flowers.

'The whole earth is our hospital', wrote T. S. Eliot in 'East Coker'; and although Larkin, unlike Eliot, accepts no religion, this poem places in

[11] Timms makes the point that this poem 'has a very complex rhyme scheme that cuts across stanza breaks': *Philip Larkin*, p. 130. F. Grubb's comment that this poem 'gives the politics of welfare a poetic, emotional justification' is well wide of the poem itself: see 'Dragons', Larkin issue of *Phoenix*, 11/12, p. 121.

perspective the human need for religion, so that the powerful religious and theological connotations of 'propitiatory'[12] draw together the religious imagery and terminology scattered through the poem. This poem builds and exhibits a vast metaphor for life; and as hospitals are the destination of every ambulance, so this poem takes the isolation and loneliness of 'Ambulances' to their logical conclusion.

A metaphor for life turns before our eyes into a metaphor for death. If death is something of an obsession in *High Windows*, however, the final poem in the collection represents Larkin's most original and enthralling treatment of the subject. Although 'The Explosion' (p. 42) deals with sudden death, it gives equal emphasis to ongoing life and vitality. The poet here does not intrude, but allows the visual imagery of the poem to comment on itself. The poem begins with a finely-realized picture of miners walking to work (the title refers to a pit explosion). One of them finds a nest of lark's eggs; and as the miners 'pass' through the 'tall gates' to their doom the poem's concentration narrows in such a way as to bring before our eyes a comprehensive and imaginative vision of both life and death. From the explosion we cut straight to the funeral service:

> *The dead go on before us, they*
> *Are sitting in God's house in comfort,*
> *We shall see them face to face—*
>
> Plain as lettering in the chapels
> It was said, and for a second
> Wives saw men of the explosion
>
> Larger than in life they managed—
> Gold as on a coin, or walking
> Somehow from the sun towards them,
>
> One showing the eggs unbroken.

Concentrated on the most solemn of human rituals, the funeral service, this vision is both providential and beneficent. The sound of the preacher's voice does come to us, italicized, as 'lettering in the chapels', from which it is but a swift and perfectly natural transition to the momentary resurrection of the dead men in the minds of their wives (not widows). Following this instantaneous unity of living and dead the poem concludes with a startling image of the continuity of nature, and it is

[12] See *OED*.

altogether fitting that the last poem in a book so concerned with ritual and continuity should leave us contemplating an image of naturalistic promise.

The unusualness of this poem (the trochaic metre recalls Longfellow's *Hiawatha*) takes us back to Larkin's comment quoted at the beginning of this chapter: 'the great thing . . . is to be different from yourself'. Many poems in this book are quite different from anything Larkin has written previously. One thinks not only of 'The Explosion', but also of 'Trees', 'The Card-Players', and of course 'Livings', the three parts of which could well be by different people. Against the fragmentation that necessarily accompanies such diversity of technical departures should be balanced an appreciation of the quality of many of the unfamiliar poems—the superb poise of 'The Trees', the boldly providential vision of 'The Explosion'—as well as an awareness of the poet's fresh approach to familiar concerns. The unconsciously ritualistic aspects of human behaviour have always fascinated Larkin, but in no other collection do we find such a sustained effort to point out the ritualistic side of familiar things. The technique of symbol and commentary that we saw extended from the self-proclaimed metaphors of *The Less Deceived* to the realistic urban scene in *The Whitsun Weddings* is here extended further to include common modes of social behaviour. Thematically, the desire for community and continuity is played hard against the isolation and loneliness that are felt by Larkin to be part of the condition of modern man. And if Larkin's intense and admitted Englishness emerges strongly in poems whose lack of distance and perspective renders them unsatisfactory, the crudeness of these public pronouncements illustrates by contrast the excellence of those poems which base themselves on localized perceptions of experience.

Again we notice a fascination with death, although death is seen as something against which life has to be measured, as well as its inevitable accompaniment. Again, too, we notice techniques familiar from previous poems, such as the visual directiveness of 'Friday Night in the Royal Station Hotel' and the dramatic organization of rhyme in 'Vers de Société'. In this collection, however, more insistent efforts are made to draw our attention to the very appearance of the printed page: '*this* page' in 'Posterity', the typographical balance between normal and italicized print in 'Sympathy in White Major', the visualized emblem of the preacher's words in 'The Explosion'. Images of windows and glass dominate this volume, and many poems use italics; for this typographical device is a technical correlative to the different perspectives and perceptions that window images are likewise used to focus. Similarly, the tension between rhyme-scheme and stanza-form in 'The Building' is

Larkin's most adroit and intriguing exploitation of a simultaneously verbal and visual pun which correlates the meaning of *stanza* with its dramatic use, which also recalls the title of the poem, and which works to entice the reader to the moral realization constructed by the poem. Once more we notice the diffuseness of the authorial presence, and as we move from the sympathetic involvement of 'Sympathy in White Major' to the mock impersonality of 'This Be The Verse' the divergent forms into which this presence is projected remind us of how much can germinate in the gap between this poet and his speakers.

Larkin has written, exquisitely, of Housman: 'Housman could never have taken Hardy's random subjects, the second-hand suit, the discarded parasol. His sorrow required its own mythology, the haunting, half-realised legend of ploughing, enlisting, betrothals and betrayals and hangings, and always behind them summertime on Bredon, the wind on Wenlock Edge, and nettles blowing on graves'.[13] Larkin himself can, like Hardy, take the random subject: the cliché, the train journey, skin, the evening under lamplight, the photograph album, the glass of water. But his sorrow also requires its own mythology: weddings, funerals, and other human rituals; the symbols and agents of consumerism and advertising; roads not taken leading away from bed-sitting rooms in lonely middle-age. And always behind them the sweeping landscape of Humberside and East Yorkshire which, in its mingling of rural and industrial, comes to stand for the random juxtaposition of beauty and beastliness which is contemporary England.

This mythology channels and generalizes. It takes us beyond the personal and the topical to a sorrow that encompasses all humanity, yet from which the pressure of personal feeling is rarely absent. Larkin's most potent effects, in *High Windows* as elsewhere, are controlled by a manner balanced finely between intimacy and impersonality, a manner calculated to draw us into the vital core of a poem. 'High Windows' leaves us utterly absorbed in its dominant image, and because of our dramatic involvement in the journey into 'The Building' we are permitted to feel that we are constructing our own interpretation of human life. Larkin's manner is such that he allows us to apprehend his insights as though they were our own. It is this, above all, which enables him to write with such compelling perception on such apparently mundane subjects, and which allows him to illuminate so thoughtfully the unthinking 'ordinariness' of so much that we do and feel.

[13] Philip Larkin, 'Love Poetry', *The Guardian Weekly*, Vol. 121, No. 20, 11 November 1979, p. 22. (Review of Richard Perceval Graves, *A. E. Housman: The Scholar-Poet*.)